MINDFULNESS FOR BEGINNERS

HOW TO STOP WORRYING, REDUCE STRESS,
OVERCOME ANXIETY, CALM YOUR MIND,
INCREASE HAPPINESS, IMPROVE FOCUS, ENJOY
YOUR LIFE AND LIVE IN THE PRESENT MOMENT

GABRIEL SHAW

1

INTRODUCTION

W hat comes to your mind when you hear the word "Mindfulness"? Do you associate the word with yoga, meditation, spirituality or people wearing suits in an office working at a computer?

IF YOU ASK most people they would generally say the former and wouldn't associate it with office workers at all however mindfulness is very broad and includes many aspects we may be unaware of.

MINDFULNESS IS INTERPRETED by different people in many ways, but at its core it is defined as the trait of focusing fully on the present moment.

MINDFULNESS WILL SIGNIFICANTLY ENHANCE every experience in your life, whether it is spending quality time with a loved one, eating your meals, studying for an exam, going for a walk or sitting down working on a computer.

.   .   .

THERE ARE countless studies scientifically showing that practicing mindfulness can enhance many areas of your life including your mental and physical well-being.

AT THE START of this book, you will learn all the basics about mindfulness and the health benefits of mindfulness as evidenced by scientific research.

IN THE CHAPTERS AFTER THAT, you will learn practical techniques on how to apply mindfulness in many aspects of your life, such as:

- Calming your mind and negative thoughts
- Reducing stress, anxiety, and depression,
- Increasing your happiness,
- Improving your relationships,
- Boosting your productivity at work

AT THE END of this book, you will find some of the best mindfulness quotes to keep you inspired and motivated to practice it as well as some recommended mindfulness apps and websites to help you nurture this habit.

THIS BOOK IS FOR ANYONE, young or old, who wants to live a more fulfilled and happier life by embracing and appreciating the present moment.

.   .   .

WHILE THIS BOOK is a short introduction, it contains a lot of practical exercises that you can apply to your life and you should not try to rush through this book but instead absorb and reflect on the information in the book.

WHILE YOU MAY LIVE A VERY busy life and feel that you can read this book while multitasking, sitting in front of TV or responding to notifications and emails when they pop up, however this is an example of not being mindful or focused.

YOU CAN START to incorporate mindful practice when reading this book by not being distracted by Facebook, emails, Television, notifications, radio, conversations or browsing the internet while reading.

YOU CAN PRACTICE mindful reading by taking the time to sit in a quiet space inside or in nature and read.

IF YOU ARE on a train or feel you don't have the time to sit and read this then you can just be mindful to not change between apps or websites while reading this book, read it in your head to yourself and try not to let your mind wander to other thoughts while reading.

Mindfulness Exercise

Practice mindfulness while reading this book.

TURN off notifications and distractions while reading. Focus on the book and the process of reading.

.   .   .

BE aware of your desire to switch between apps or respond to notifications, resist and bring your attention back to the book.

NOTICE your mind wander to other thoughts as you are reading and bring your attention back to the words.

2

WHAT IS MINDFULNESS?

"The best way to capture moments is to pay attention. This is how we cultivate mindfulness. Mindfulness means being awake. It means knowing what you are doing." - Jon Kabat-Zinn

You have most likely heard of the word "mindfulness" in at least one point of your life. It is being talked about online, in television shows, and perhaps among friends. But what is mindfulness, really?

Mindlessness is the opposite of mindfulness and in order to understand the benefits of mindfulness, it helps to understand what mindlessness is and why it is so detrimental.

Mindlessness is not being aware of what you are doing, not paying attention to what you are doing and performing tasks and actions without your mind being present on the activity you are doing.

You may have sat down to do an important task at 9am; then, without thinking opened a new browser window, checked Facebook, checked emails, then read an article online and lost focus and forgotten what you were going to work on in the first place. By the time you remember what you were meant to work on, an hour has gone past and you feel like you've been busy but you haven't achieved anything. Your mind and attention has been mindlessly wandering and not focusing.

Another example of mindlessness is when you are talking to someone but your mind is wandering - perhaps you are thinking about all the things you need to get done that day - and your thoughts are elsewhere and not on what the person is saying. They then ask you a question, snapping you back to focus and you need to apologize that you weren't listening and missed what they were saying.

Mindless eating is another example. You sit down for dinner in front of the TV, you are distracted by TV and watching a show and eat your food quickly without even noticing the taste or what you are eating. You consume whatever is on your plate without thought to the food or taste. Afterwards you may even forget what you ate for dinner or when the last time you ate was because you are doing it mindlessly.

Forgetting things is often not a sign of forgetfulness or memory loss but of mindlessness. You may have rushed out of the house in a hurry only to realize after it's too late and that you had forgotten something important.

You may find that no matter how many times you tell yourself to remember that item the day before, you still forget it. You may blame a bad memory but in fact, it's likely you do your morning routine in a hurry, without thinking, and any changes to this routine are not considered as you're just mindlessly going through the motions without thinking.

You may have spent the morning going over a conversation you're going to have in the future with your boss or staff member but you are mindlessly focusing on the future instead of the present moment. This causes your mind to not be aware of your present situation and surroundings, causing distraction and mindlessness as you go about your tasks.

What makes mindfulness so interesting yet so profound to a lot of people is that it is so simple. In its very core, mindfulness is about paying full attention to the present moment – your task at hand, your current responsibilities, your thoughts, feelings, physical sensations, and so on.

Some people often complain that they simply cannot be mindful because their mind is too restless. This may be the reason why so many give up on mindfulness meditation after one or two sessions. However, mindfulness is not about "stopping" the thoughts in your mind.

Rather, mindfulness is about becoming fully aware of them without associating yourself with them. As acclaimed author Paolo Coelho once wrote: *"thoughts are like wild horses. Let them run wild in your mind as you observe from a distance. Eventually, they will wear themselves out."* This is an excellent metaphor for mindfulness.

Mindfulness is not a new concept, the practice of mindfulness dates back thousands of years to the original practices of Buddhism. However, while mindfulness has origins in Buddhism, you do not have to become a Buddhist to practice mindfulness.

In the original practices of mindfulness, people practiced meditation techniques such as Vipassana as they are said to help enhance awareness and establish a connection with the Four Foundations, namely the body, the feelings, the mind, and the phenomena of the universe.

The understanding is that lack of mindful concentration causes suffering. This is mainly because most of us are not in touch with the present moment but rather attached to things that are deemed as "impermanent" – memories from the past, emotions towards someone, material things, and so on.

Mindfulness enables one to gain insight into the true nature of reality, which is defined as impermanence, suffering, and insight, or the Three Marks of Existence. Through understanding these three, one can free oneself from suffering and fear.

Through mindfulness, a person can overcome these stressors simply by focusing on what is "real," which is what is happening in the present moment. It enables the person to take a step back from all the chaos to think in a nonjudgmental, non-attached, and open-minded way.

As mentioned, while Buddhists practice mindfulness, you do not need to practice any Buddhist teachings to use mindfulness in everyday life. In fact, an increasing number of scientific evidences reveal that the practice of secular mindfulness can help manage stress and improve overall health.

There is plenty of scientific research supporting these claims, and we will get to those in the succeeding chapters, but when you stop to think about it, it makes a lot of sense.

After all, people in the modern times have become too caught up with their everyday stressors, whether it is a part of the environment such as heavy traffic, or something more internal such as rumination of past regrets or future worries.

Think about times in your life when you've been stressed or unhappy - not by your present experience but by thoughts of the future or of the past. You may have been with a friend or loved one at dinner, a park, or a nice relaxing environment and yet you were not enjoying the present moment as your thoughts were racing, causing you unease and unhappiness about future or past events.

How Mindfulness Works

To help you develop a clearer picture of what being mindful is, here are the two fundamental steps that psychologists use to explain mindfulness in therapy:

Step 1: Use your five senses to engage with your environment.

Our senses of sight, smell, hearing, touch, and taste are our direct way of taking in everything around us. By allowing the mind to be filled with stimuli purely based on them, we could immediately get in touch with what is currently happening around us.

For instance, look around you and notice the different colors, shapes, and sizes that you can see. Smell the scents wafting in the air. As you inhale, notice how the air feels inside your body. Observe the taste inside your mouth, or the lack of taste. Reach out and touch the object closest to you, paying attention to how it feels against your skin.

Step 2: Acknowledge the thoughts in your mind with acceptance and without judgement.

As you interact with your environment, you cannot help but notice your mind drifting from the initial sensations to thoughts that would judge or even criticize whatever it is you are sensing. These are called "automatic thoughts" and they are completely normal, of course.

In mindfulness, you learn not to dwell on those thoughts, but instead to think of them merely as impermanent bubbles that pop up and then dissolve.

For example, you start thinking about someone who had hurt your feelings in the past. Instead of dwelling on that thought and thinking about why or how that happened or what could have been different, you need to become detached from the memory as if you are a mere onlooker. Let the memory take its natural course until it fades away, kind of like a cloud passing you by.

It can be quite challenging not to react upon those thoughts, which is why mindfulness takes practice.

These two steps are typically applied in meditation as a form of therapy. Be that as it may, mindfulness is not just practiced during meditation. In fact, it is encouraged in everyday life. For instance, you can become more mindful while you are eating, doing your household chores, and exercising (you will learn more about these later).

Mindfulness can be practiced by anyone anywhere and at any time of the day. Those who practice it daily swear that it has helped them improve their performance at work, enhance their relationships, and boost their overall mental and physical health. It has prevented them from acting on their emotions, thus sparing them from potentially dangerous, embarrassing, and other regrettable situations.

Aside from these, there are many more benefits to mindfulness. You can learn more about them in the next three chapters.

Mindfulness Exercise

Focus on reducing distractions and building attention

·   ·   ·

IN THE PREVIOUS CHAPTER, you were asked to focus on being mindful when reading by turning off notifications and being aware when your mind wanders or wants to be distracted.

HAVE you noticed your mind wandering? Are you having trouble focusing on reading without changing between apps or multitasking?

BUY A SMALL NOTEPAD AND PEN, when you are reading, notice when your mind wanders or you have a desire to do something else. Don't change or respond to the desire. Take a note on the notepad and bring your attention back to the book.

MINDFULNESS IS ABOUT AWARENESS, attention and being present. Your mind will constantly be thinking of things to do, emails to respond to, shopping items and you may feel they are urgent or you must respond to them immediately before you forget.

THIS LEADS to distraction from your initial focus and takes longer than expected, often leading to a series of additional distractions until you forgot what you were originally doing.

HAVING A NOTEPAD AND PEN, allows you to write down the distraction without being pulled away from your current focus. You can then bring your focus back to your current task knowing you won't forget that thought and will be able to deal with it later.

3

THE HEALTH BENEFITS OF MINDFULNESS

"Pure awareness transcends thinking. It allows you to step outside the chattering negative self-talk and your reactive impulses and emotions.

IT ALLOWS *you to look at the world once again with open eyes. And when you do so, a sense of wonder and quiet contentment begins to reappear in your life.*" - Mark Williams

MINDFULNESS IS one of the major buzzwords recently, mainly because it has scientifically proven health benefits. Companies such as Apple, Google, Nike, Proctor & Gamble, and HBO have even been sponsoring mindfulness meditation sessions for their employees because it enhances productivity, problem solving skills, creativity, and overall health.

INDEED, mindfulness does more than just help you get in touch with the present moment. By making it a daily habit, you will be able to reap the following health benefits that can improve your physical and mental health and possibly even your quality of life.

MINDFULNESS REDUCES **stress**

MOST OF US know that chronic stress weakens the immune system and increases one's risk of developing chronic inflammation, the root of all diseases. Therefore, it is important to manage our stress levels, and the good thing is that mindfulness meditation can decrease the cortisol levels in the blood, or the hormone responsible for causing the symptoms of stress.

ACCORDING to a 2013 study published in *Health Psychology,* the cortisol levels of its participants decreased significantly after they underwent a mindfulness retreat that involved mindful breathing, and positive thought meditation.

Mindfulness reduces risk of depression

One of the main reasons why scientists examined the subject of mindfulness is that it has helped many people – especially pregnant women and teens – cope with anxiety and depression.

FOR INSTANCE, a study involving pregnant women who were at high risk of developing postnatal depression revealed that prenatal mindfulness yoga significantly decreased their stress levels. It has even helped decrease their risk of preterm labor and pregnancy-triggered hypertension. The study was published in the 2012 issue of *Complementary Therapies in Clinical Practice.*

MINDFULNESS PROGRAMS in schools have also helped teens cope with depression-related symptoms. A 2014 study published in an issue of

Mindfulness revealed that in-class mindfulness training programs decreased the symptoms of anxiety, stress, and depression among its adolescent participants.

Mindfulness improves your quality of sleep

IN 2015, the World Health Organization declared that there may be a link between sleep deprivation and heart disease. If you are one of those who often find themselves having trouble falling or staying asleep at night, then mindfulness meditation can help you.

A STUDY PUBLISHED in the April 2015 issue of *JAMA Internal Medicine* revealed that the participants who underwent mindful awareness practices, especially mindfulness meditation, experienced significant improvement in their quality of sleep. Specifically, the symptoms related to insomnia, depression, fatigue, stress, and anxiety declined because of the intervention.

Mindfulness can help you stick to your weight loss regimen

IF YOU ARE WORKING on shedding off excess weight through diet and exercise, then you can incorporate mindfulness into your regimen so that you are more likely to achieve your fitness goals.

ACCORDING to a study published in the 2015 issue of *Psychosomatic Medicine*, those who combined mindfulness-based interventions with their weight loss program reported significant weight loss after their program compared to those who did not incorporate mindfulness into their program.

.   .   .

THESE SCIENTIFICALLY PROVEN health benefits of mindfulness make a
very convincing case to start building the habit of mindfulness meditation. However, aside from the benefits of being able to reduce your
stress levels, lower your risk of depression, enhance the quality of
your sleep, and even aid in your weight loss program, there are even
more benefits to mindfulness as you will soon learn in the next
chapter.

Mindfulness Exercise
Be aware of mindlessness actions done on autopilot

THERE ARE SO many tasks that we do every day on autopilot without
thinking. There's nothing wrong with doing tasks on autopilot sometimes; in fact, repeating a task until it becomes a habit and you can do
it without thinking can be good if it's a positive task and habit.
However, we also do bad tasks and habits mindlessly without
thinking.

PICK some tasks during the day that you do automatically and then
do them with the opposite hand or a different way.

Some ideas and examples are:

- Change the hand you brush your teeth with
- Try signing your name or writing with the other hand
- Take a different route to work or home
- Take the stairs instead of the elevator

THESE TASKS that we do on autopilot do require a lot of effort and
action that we don't think about on a daily basis. Often, we brush our

teeth, then later forget if we did or not as we're doing them mindlessly or our thoughts were distracted.

BY CHANGING ACTIONS, such as the hand you use when doing tasks you usually don't think about, you become more aware of the task and the action and effort required. It makes you very aware of the action and helps you concentrate more on the action.

You don't have to do this all the time; you can go back to the way you usually do things. It's just an exercise in being aware of how automatically we often go through life.

4

THE BENEFITS OF MINDFULNESS ON YOUR MIND

"*The practice of mindfulness begins in the small, remote cave of your unconscious mind and blossoms with the sunlight of your conscious life, reaching far beyond the people and places you can see.*" - Earon Davis

Mindfulness is all about conditioning the mind to be more aware of the present moment. But how exactly does that benefit the mind? We'll go into more detail in this chapter and cover ways about how mindfulness can positively benefit the mind.

Mindfulness enhances working memory

We rely on our working memory to perform the task in front of us, interact with those around us, and process just about any information we come across throughout our day. However, there are times when our working memory fails us, especially if our mind starts to wander while in the middle of a task.

You may have encountered time when someone was talking to you and you didn't hear what they were saying because you were distracted by your thoughts. There may also have been times where you found yourself forgetting your keys or important items when you leave the house, forgetting that you left the oven or stove on in the kitchen, or losing focus while taking an important exam. Many of these we put down to being forgetful, but often, we forget to do these because we're not being mindful, we lose focus and are distracted.

If you find yourself struggling to focus, then mindfulness can enhance that skill through practice. A research report published in the 2013 issue of *Psychological Science* revealed that mindfulness training enhances the mind's working memory and at the same time decreases the mind from wandering. According to the results of the study, the 2-week mindfulness training program enhanced the participants' reading comprehension and overall ability to focus while taking the GRE or Graduate Record Examination.

Improved Attention & Focus

Do you find that your mind tends to leave you every now and again? Research has shown that after mindfulness and meditation training, participants were able to keep their focus on tasks they previously classed as being very boring. This was also found by students who needed to perform under stress.

The studies have found that those who practice meditation and mindfulness have a thicker prefrontal cortex. A larger prefrontal cortex has a direct positive correlation with cognitive ability, especially in old age for people who have practiced mindfulness and meditation for many years.

Emotional Resilience

Emotional resilience is the ability to adapt to stressful situations or overcome setbacks. People with higher levels of emotional resilience can adapt to difficult situations, overcome obstacles, manage stress and significant life changes.

Studies into mindfulness have also shown people who regularly practice mindfulness and meditation have stronger emotional resilience.

As you practice more, you may find you have better control over your emotional intelligence and resilience when dealing with difficult situations or negative emotions.

Dealing with Pain

Studies have shown that meditation and mindfulness can dramatically reduce pain signals in the brain. In one experiment, there was a 40% reduction in pain intensity and almost 60% reduction in unpleasantness of the pain.

Pain is caused by signals to the brain, as meditation and mindfulness involve controlling the brain and thoughts, it can help reduce the impact and your reaction to these pain signals.

Attention Deficit Hyperactivity Disorder (ADHD)

In a study done with ADHD patients, it was found that Mindfulness-based Cognitive Therapy (MBCT) helped reduce their hyperactivity without medication. Mindfulness contributed to a reduction in the impulsiveness in their everyday actions. The patients involved in mindfulness therapy were able to increase their awareness skills and reduce their overall symptoms of ADHD.

Empathy

Studies have shown that mindfulness can help increase not only positive emotions but compassion toward other people. When you love yourself, you can begin to love others as well. When you can accept others into your life, this will decrease your chances of suffering from social isolation. By practicing mindfulness, this can open the opportunity for social connection and result in an overall increase in positive emotions.

Mindfulness enables us to understand ourselves better

Can you imagine being able to take a step back and assess who we are in an objective way? It seems difficult, since we tend to be either biased towards our own personalities or overly negative. Yet it is important to know our true selves, otherwise we would never grow and learn. Those who fail to know themselves often end up destroying many relationships, losing opportunities in life, and ending up with depression and anxiety.

However, with mindfulness you can learn to let go of self-bias and self-criticism and get to know your true personality. A study published in 2013 in *Perspectives on Psychological Science* revealed that there is a link between self-knowledge and mindfulness.

According to the researcher, Erika Carlson, mindfulness can break down the two major barriers to knowing one's true self, namely the informational barriers (or the quality and quantity of information a person has about him or herself) and the motivational barriers (or the motives that affect how a person understands and responds to the information he has about him or herself).

Mindfulness reduces your tendency to ruminate

Rumination in the broadest sense of the word refers to a "calm, lengthy, and intent consideration," but in Psychology it refers to the compulsion of putting too much attention on one's source of stress instead of concentrating on a solution. One example of rumination is when you keep thinking about a mistake you had made in the past and how things could happen differently if only you did not commit it.

Many people suffer from constant rumination, so much so that it negatively affects the state of their mind and quality of life. If you constantly find yourself ruminating, then it may be beneficial to turn to mindfulness. Multiple studies can attest to the effectiveness of mindfulness in reducing rumination. One study, published in a 2009 issue of *The Journal of Science and Healing,* revealed that the adult participants who completed the Mindfulness-Based Stress Reduction (MBSR) training showed a decrease in symptoms of depression as well as rumination.

When we exercise, over time we see tangible changes to our physical body. Mindfulness can be considered as exercise for the brain that also takes a lot of training and practice.

While the results can not be see physically on your body and they do take time. Don't be discouraged, there are numerous benefits of mindfulness on the mind. Consistent daily practice, bringing yourself into the present, improving your concentration and focus will have a noticeable impact on your mind and your life.

Mindfulness exercise

Mindful appreciation of things you take for granted

In the last exercise, you focused on actions that you usually don't notice at all or think about when you're doing them.

In this exercise, you are going to pay attention to some things that you generally don't think about.

For example, you may be reading this on a phone, eBook reader or tablet, but have you stopped to think about what went into this in order for you to be able to read this on that device.

The device was once an idea in someone's head, they worked with a team to design and create it, then all the bits of metal and plastic that had to be put together. The software that was written by someone for it to run, the shipping of it from a factory to a warehouse or store, the invention of electricity to power the device, the power plant that powers the electrical grid to charge it.

If you ordered it online and it was delivered to you, have you thought about the postal system and how that was created, the systems in place to receive the package, scan it through to the correct country, city and suburb, then the postal worker, that brings it out for delivery after it has travelled all that distance across the world and country.

Have you ever thought about how fresh water comes to you when you turn on a tap and the people, machines and processes behind it? How far it travels before it reaches your home?

Think about some other processes in your life that you usually take for granted, think about how it comes into your life and all the processes and people behind it to bring it to you.

Notice the finer details of those things and take time to examine and notice them in detail.

Think about how they are connected and all the people, machines, animals and processes connected in making or bring them to you.

Think about what your life might be like without those things.

5

CALMING YOUR MIND AND THOUGHTS THROUGH MINDFULNESS

"*You can't stop the waves, but you can learn to surf.*" - Jon Kabat-Zinn

THE MIND CAN BE VERY a hyperactive at times. There are times when all that buzz serves a strong purpose, such as when you are trying to solve a problem, stirring up your creative juices, or experiencing a lot of strong emotions because of a major life experience or two.

However, it is not healthy for the mind to be too restless for it could lead to stress and anxiety that cause more harm than good in the long run. A hyperactive mind can be especially annoying when you are trying to fall asleep. During the times when you need to relax and calm your mind, mindfulness can be a big help.

TO CALM the mind and let go of overwhelming thoughts through mindfulness, here are some techniques you can try:

. . .

GET in touch with your senses

WHEN THE MIND is filled with unhelpful thoughts, it helps to redirect its attention towards the senses instead. Clinical psychologist Elisha Goldstein calls this special technique the Practice 3x3. To do it, you must first focus on three of your five senses (such as your sense of sight, sound, and smell). Focus on them one at a time and each time you do, notice what you immediately pick up with that sense.

FOR EXAMPLE, let us say your mind is too filled with "planning and worrying" thoughts as you lay in bed that night. Once you notice that you are thinking too much, shift your focus towards your sense of hearing. What do you hear? What kind of sound is it? Would you be able to describe it? Then spend time on that sense for a while.

After that, you can shift to your sense of smell. Do you smell anything? If you do, what kind of scent is it? If you don't, how do you describe the absence of smell? And so on.

GIVE the Practice this 3x3 technique a try and you will notice that it redirects your focus towards your present moment and helps quell down the stress or anxiety caused by your own mind.

PRACTICE SELF-COMPASSION

STRESSFUL SITUATIONS CAUSE pain and anxiety and, while this can be painful at the time, it is these painful situations that allow us to better appreciate other moments in our life. When you experience pain and anxiety it helps to acknowledge it when you feel it and to accept that you are feeling it. Being mindful of painful and stressful feelings, you would then be able to move on towards releasing those thoughts that come with those feelings.

REMEMBER THAT EVERYONE, rich or poor, experiences pain and an overactive mind. By recognizing that you are not alone in your state you will feel more compassionate towards yourself.

A PRACTICAL WAY TO exercise self-compassion is become curious with the sensations happening inside your mind. Does your mind feel heavy? Let the thoughts wear themselves out. Don't dwell on the thoughts, just let them pass. Remember your thoughts are not you.

IF YOU ARE EXPERIENCING negative thoughts and worrying about the future, think about what you would say to a close friend if they had the same issues. Would you be dwelling on things going wrong and telling them all the negative thoughts you are telling yourself? Think about how you would reassure your friend, the positive things you would say to them. Then say them to yourself, don't beat yourself up, don't focus on the negative outcomes. Practice the same compassion and positive reassurance you would show to a friend.

Write your thoughts down

WHEN OUR MIND is hyperactive it seems like you have a million thoughts every second. It's hard to shut our mind off when it seems there are so many problems and issues things to think about. The mind works fast - each thought can be a fraction of a second - and the mind then continues to repeat the same negative thoughts or worries making it seem like there is too much going on.

· · ·

THIS LEADS TO STRESS, anxiety and the feeling of being overwhelmed by everything we have going on.

HOWEVER, if you take a pen to paper when you can't calm your thoughts then your mind is forced to think at the same pace as you can write.

TRY to write out all your thoughts. Don't try and structure them, just free write them and let the thoughts flow onto the paper. It might seem difficult to get started but just start writing whatever comes to your mind and keep writing until you can't write anymore.

EVENTUALLY, you will run out of things to write, it may take a few pages or even longer, but once you've finished everything in your head will be on paper. Even if you have been thinking about these thoughts for hours, you will find less than 30 minutes is usually enough time to get these thoughts out of your head and onto paper to clearly see your thought patterns and be mindful of why this is worrying you.

ASIDE FROM THESE TECHNIQUES, you will learn plenty of other ways to use mindfulness for relaxation. The next chapter, in fact, will delve even deeper into the subject of mindfulness as it relates to stress and anxiety.

Mindfulness exercise

Being mindful of your senses

In the last couple of exercises, you became more aware and mindful of tasks, things and process you generally don't notice on a daily basis.

In this exercise, you'll focus on being more mindful of your senses and experience in the moment.

Wherever you are right now, focus on your senses, ask and answer the below questions.

Remember to pay careful attention, answer slowly and name more than one thing for each question.

What can I hear at this moment?

What can I see at this moment?

What can I feel at this moment?

6

MINDFULNESS TO REDUCE ANXIETY AND STRESS

"*I*n this moment, there is plenty of time. In this moment, you are precisely as you should be. In this moment, there is infinite possibility." - Victoria Moran

Everybody has experienced a form of stress or anxiety at some point in their life. Some people experience it more severely than others including panic attacks involving heart palpitations, sweaty palms, shortness of breath, and an overall sense of panic when facing distressing situations.

Regardless of the severity of symptoms you may experience, it can have serious detrimental effects on your life. In this chapter, we will explore some ways mindfulness can help deal with stress and anxiety.

Stress is defined as a state of mental or emotional strain, while anxiety is a more severe or permanent state of worry and nervousness that can be much more serious. While feeling stressed or anxious every now and then is a completely normal part of everyday life, it is an altogether different story when you experience it almost every day.

In fact, chronic stress and anxiety are now regarded as serious illnesses that need to be addressed as early as possible. Otherwise, it could lead to the development of debilitating diseases and clinical depression. According to a survey by the World Health Organization, one in every fifty people experience generalized anxiety, or the state of feeling anxious throughout the waking day, at least once in their life.

Thankfully, we all have free access to the therapeutic benefits of mindfulness to reduce everyday stress levels and anxiety. However, it is important to note that mindfulness should be regarded as *supplemental* rather than as an alternative to the more conventional way of treating anxiety and stress. It is always best to consult a licensed therapist and to combine mindfulness with proper diet and exercise to significantly lower anxiety and stress levels.

Let us now look at how you can use mindfulness to remain calm and composed while facing stressful situations:

Understanding the Source of Anxiety and Stress

Anxiety and stress are caused by a broad range of factors. Some people are genetically predisposed to be more susceptible to anxiety, while others have gone through experiences in life that caused anxiety to develop with trigger events. For most, if not all, certain situations can trigger stress and anxiety: a project that is overdue, financial problems, relationship issues, and so on. All too often, anxiety and stress are aggravated by certain substances, such as recreational drugs and caffeine.

Sometimes we become so overwhelmed by the feeling of fear itself that we are not able to address the root of the problem. However, the only way to let go of the fear is to determine why it surfaces in the first place. This can be quite a challenging thing to do, which is why people usually prefer to avoid or block out the source of their fear.

A common example of avoiding one's source of stress is through procrastination. Instead of dealing with the source of stress, the person would usually turn to less important but more engaging activities. This might provide temporary relief, but in the long run the source of stress would only resurface once more and then the cycle continues.

Through mindfulness, you can break the cycle of stress and anxiety by acknowledging the feelings as they occur. This might sound counterintuitive, especially given the fact that their physical, emotional, and psychological symptoms are downright unhealthy. However, by accepting the fact that you are experiencing stress and anxiety, you will eventually be able to move on to dealing with them in a more curious and constructive way rather than through avoidance.

Mindfulness Meditation for Stress and Anxiety

IT IS important to understand that mindfulness is not about eliminating stress and anxiety forever. It is not also about getting rid of the negative thought, memory, or experience that is the source of your stress. Rather, it is about developing the right mindset towards the inevitable moments in life that can trigger stress. Through practice, you will be able to break free from being overcome by rumination and instead adopt a constructive, curious, and helpful attitude towards stress.

THE BEST PART is that just about any type of mindfulness meditation or other technique can help you reduce stress and anxiety. But if you are looking for an exercise you can practice regularly to help you cope with stress and anxiety as soon as they strike, then here are the steps:

STEP 1: Sit or lie down comfortably in a private place where no one will disturb you. Keep your back straight and shoulders relaxed, welcoming a strong, relaxed self-confidence.

STEP 2: Calmly answer each of the following questions:

What do I see? Hear? Smell? Taste? Touch?
What physical sensations am I noticing?
What are my emotions?
What are my thoughts?

Take your time in formulating your response to each of them. Allow yourself to be as descriptive as you can possibly be.

STEP 3: After answering each of the questions, stay in tune with the present moment for a few minutes. Do not attempt to change anything, but simply allow it to be as it is. Acknowledge their presence and accept them as part of your present moment.

STEP 4: As soon as you are ready, you may place your hand on top of your abdomen. Release the tension from your hand and allow it to rise and fall with your belly as you inhale and exhale. Bring your focus entirely on your hand and belly as it serves as your core.

WHEN YOU NOTICE worrisome or stressful thoughts start to creep into your mind, acknowledge them to be there, but do not dwell on them. Instead, gently draw your attention back to your core, which is what is happening in the present moment.

STEP 5: After a few minutes of sustained focus on your abdomen, gently broaden your awareness towards your entire body as you continue to breath. Notice the sensations you feel throughout your body each time you inhale and exhale. Each time your mind starts to ruminate on thoughts unrelated to the present moment, simply draw it back again.

. . .

STEP 6: Become aware of the calm feeling that is in this present moment. Acknowledge that you are alive, well, and breathing. Accept stress and anxiety as momentary, that the thoughts, emotions, and physical sensations associated to them may arise but will also fade away.

OTHER TECHNIQUES TO **reduce stress and anxiety**

WHAT WORKS for one person might not work for another, the mind is complex and each person has a unique mind and thoughts that react differently to certain techniques.

IN THE PREVIOUS CHAPTER, there were some techniques for calming the mind, these can also be used for reducing stress and anxiety.

THE TECHNIQUE of writing your thoughts - what you are worried about, why you are worried about that, what is the worst that can happen, what is within your control, what is out of your control and what action you can take - can help you slow your thoughts and address the thoughts in a calm logical way.

IF YOU CAN'T STOP your mind from running off to different thoughts, then writing down the questions and answers to what your emotions and thoughts are, along with your sense and physical sensations, can be a useful first step to calm your mind down to a more reasonable speed you can manage.

THERE IS a metaphor which likens thoughts to horses in a field: if you chase them they will run faster, if you attempt to ride them or to tame them then you will not be in control of where they take you. It is best to just observe them from a distance and let them wear themselves out.

WRITING your thoughts with whatever comes to mind, is a form of observing your thoughts on paper; eventually the thoughts will wear themselves out and you will have captured them all on paper. This can be especially useful at night when you can't sleep due to a racing mind.

THE REASON this writing technique is recommended is that when you experience stress and anxiety, it can be very difficult to calm your mind and thoughts with meditation, mindfulness or breathing techniques. It is very difficult at the start and your mind needs to reach a level of calm first which can be helped by writing.

ONCE YOU HAVE FELT some calm in your mind though techniques that work for you, then building a meditation habit will help build upon this and help you gain greater calm.

KEEP PRACTICING this short mindfulness exercise regularly, preferably in the mornings so that you can start your day with a mindful and calm attitude. Later, during those moments when you start to feel stressed or anxious, you will learn to stay grounded on your core and not let the negativity overwhelm you.

Mindfulness exercise

Writing to ease worry and racing thoughts

As described above, writing out your thoughts, emotions and anything that is racing around in your mind can help get these thoughts onto paper and calm your mind.

A pen and paper is recommended as it will be easier to concentrate and you are less likely to feel the urge to switch between apps. If you don't have a pen paper, then you can use a writing app or program.

Write down your thoughts and emotions: how you're feeling and why. It doesn't have to be structured, just write it down as it comes to mind.

If you're struggling to get started or don't have any racing thoughts, write down what you need to do, people you need to contact, tasks you need to work on this week, errands to run, bills to pay etc.

Write whatever is on your mind and get your to do list, people you need to contact, most important tasks and shopping list out of your mind and onto paper.

Capture everything you can and get it out of your head.

Once you have it out of your mind and thoughts, relax and tell yourself that you don't need to worry about things, they are captured in a place you can refer to them.

Take 10 deep breaths in and out, counting 1 as you breathe in and 2 as you breathe out.

Often a lot of stress and anxiety comes from feeling overwhelmed - we have so much to do, we don't know where to start and there's not enough time.

We also go over the same thoughts in our head in rapid succession, ruminating on bad thoughts, things we should have said to people, things we are angry or annoyed about. Getting these out of your mind and onto paper often removes or reduces the emotions associated with them as well that we experience by constantly repeating them in our mind.

Note: As previously mentioned, mindfulness and meditation are supplementary activities for stress and anxiety. The symptoms can be quite serious and it's recommended that you consult professionals regarding your individual condition and requirements.

7

MINDFULNESS TO REDUCE DEPRESSION

"The way to live in the present is to remember that 'This too shall pass.'

WHEN YOU EXPERIENCE JOY, remembering that 'This too shall pass' helps you savor the here and now.

WHEN YOU EXPERIENCE pain and sorrow, remembering that 'This too shall pass' reminds you that grief, like joy, is only temporary." - Joey Green

IF YOU, at any point in your life, have ever experienced feeling inadequate and uninspired to the point of giving up, or thinking that life is not worth living, then you are not alone. Depression affects over 300 million people all over the world, making it a serious health concern as classed by the World Health Organization.

. . .

DEPRESSION SHOULD NEVER BE TAKEN LIGHTLY and should not be excused merely as "prolonged sadness." The symptoms of depression are real and are, in fact, considered to be an illness.

You can tell whether you are depressed if you consistently have low energy, are in a low mood, cannot focus on anything, and do not find interest or pleasure in anything. You may also find it either difficult to sleep or that you sleep off most of the day. Your appetite also changes when you are depressed – you either lose it or it goes on overdrive.

IF YOU ARE DEPRESSED, do not be afraid to seek guidance and support from a health professional, because you can get past this experience and move on to a much better quality of life. On the other hand, if you have experienced being depressed before and you want to decrease the chance of it recurring, then you can use mindfulness as an additional technique with a depression management plan.

UNDERSTANDING What Triggers Depression

SADNESS BEGINS with negative thoughts and emotions. Often, these lead to feeling less motivated to do anything. However, scientists explain that one's sadness can spiral into depression because of two main causes. The first is called Experiential Avoidance and the second is Rumination.

EXPERIENTIAL AVOIDANCE IS when you try to always avoid anything that is negative or unpleasant. You try to escape from the emotions that are clearly there, leaving them to be unresolved.

.   .   .

RUMINATION, as mentioned earlier, is when you continue to replay negative thoughts in your mind constantly. When a person ruminates, they attempt to formulate answers out of probabilities. This causes them to feel emotions and reactions as though they have happened or continue to happen again even though they are merely products of their own thoughts.

THE ONLY WAY TO escape these two causes is by acknowledging them when they take place. It is important to recognize that you are avoiding the problem or ruminating over it. This can be achieved through mindfulness.

MINDFULNESS TO PREVENT Depression

IF YOU ARE ALREADY in an emotional slump, your best course of action is to seek professional guidance. However, if you notice that you are simply in a low mood but can still recover from it on your own, then you can apply the following steps to keep yourself from falling into depression:

STEP 1: Start by becoming aware of the part of your body where you feel negative emotion can be felt most strongly.

Some people feel a tightness in their chest, while others experience an upset stomach. Whichever body part it is where the negative emotion is manifesting, approach the sensation in a curious, non-judgmental manner. You may observe it as if you are a spectator tasked to describe it without criticism.

STEP 2: Concentrate fully on that part of your body in which you feel the most negative energy caused by your low mood. As you continue to breathe in and out, notice how each in- and out-breath affects that part of your body. Does it feel uncomfortable or does it start to fade away with each breath?

DO NOT ATTEMPT to change the sensation you feel in that body part. Rather, acknowledge the sensation and be okay with it being there.

STEP 3: Accept that you are more than that part of your body. Be like a mere spectator of what is happening to that sensation. What kind of thoughts come across your mind because of the sensation? Do the same thoughts recur or do they rapidly shift? If you notice this, then your mind may be in a state of Rumination. If so, then let your thoughts run wild but do not engage with them. Let them wear themselves out.

STEP 4: Observe whether you feel a desire to eliminate the negative sensation, thought, or emotion. If you do, then it is possible that your mind is shifting towards Experiential Avoidance. As you notice of this taking place, try to encourage your mind to be more accepting towards the negative sensation instead of avoiding it. Do not worry if you are only able to accept it halfway or even less; what matters is that you are aware of having the tendency to avoid the negative sensation.

STEP 5: By now, you have acknowledged and accepted your current state of having a low mood. At this point, you can transition towards a short, 3- to 5-minute mindful breathing meditation. This will help you to become more in tune with what is happening in the present moment.

· · ·

PRACTICING **self compassion**

IF YOU HAVE SUFFERED DEPRESSION, it can seem like the negative thoughts won't stop and it's impossible to see the positive. You may feel you have no control over your thoughts and they are constantly judging and being critical of you. You become your own worst enemy as your mind continues a negative spiral that you find you can't escape from.

PRACTICING self compassion can help reduce negative thoughts by being aware of your thoughts and how you speak to yourself to change that from a negative spiral to a positive pattern.

WHEN CHANGING negative self-talk and thoughts, understand that other people feel the same way that you do, you are not alone and there are many people who have felt the same way in the past or currently feel the same way now. There are lots of support networks and people to talk to, you are not alone in your experience and feelings and don't have to deal with this yourself.

DEPRESSION MAY BE CAUSED by something that happened to you in the past or something that you did and regret. You may continue to replay this in your mind and think about how things could have gone differently. You can forgive yourself the decisions you made or actions you took, accept yourself and love yourself for who you are. Tell yourself that you forgive and accept yourself and that you love yourself. The Buddhify App has guided lessons on difficult emotions that can help with this.

.   .   .

THINK about how you would talk to a friend if they had the same negative self-talk and doubts. Think about what you would say to them to comfort them and practice treating yourself like a friend. Reassuring yourself with positive thoughts like you would a friend.

GRATITUDE

PRACTICING gratitude for what you have can be powerful in helping you focus on the positives instead of the negatives. We take a lot of life for granted and are unaware that most the world's population struggles to survive, many people don't have access to water, food, shelter or basic necessities. Being grateful for what you have, no matter how small can help change negative thoughts.

GRATITUDE IS COVERED in more detail in the next chapter.

MINDFULNESS BASED COGNITIVE Therapy (MBCT)

MINDFULNESS-BASED cognitive therapy (MBCT) is a program to help prevent relapses of depression. It is specifically designed for people who have experienced major depression and is different from other mindfulness therapies that are broader.

MBCT COMBINES traditional cognitive behavioral therapy methods with mindfulness and meditation. Cognitive based therapy educates the participant about depression and traditional methods to manage it. Mindfulness and meditation is in addition to this, helping to deal with negative thoughts, feelings, doubts, rumination and self-criticism.

. . .

RUMINATION on negative thoughts and external factors can trigger a relapse of depression and MBCT helps with techniques to deal with these negative thought patterns and how to react to them. In the UK, MBCT has been endorsed as effective treatment with research showing a 50% reduction in relapses of depression. It is most effective with people who have had several relapses as a management strategy.

MINDFULNESS THERAPY HAS ALSO BEEN SHOWN to be effective in managing addiction to drugs, alcohol, gambling and other addictions. Mindfulness helps you to be aware of the cravings but not react automatically to them. Mindfulness therapy helps strengthen the prefrontal cortex allowing greater self-control of emotions and reactions.

OTHER TECHNIQUES TO help calm negative thoughts

THIS BOOK COVERS a wide range of mindfulness exercises. There are techniques for work, to calm your mind and increase happiness. Different techniques will have different results for each person, a technique could be effective for one person but not for someone else.

ALONG WITH THE information listed in this chapter, there are a range of other techniques throughout the book to try which may be more effective.

REMEMBER that mindfulness doesn't change the problems you are facing, you will still need to take action or consult professionals. However, mindfulness will help you respond to situations better, feeling less overwhelmed and not dwelling on negative thoughts and feelings.

THE MORE YOU practice these exercises each time you are in a low mood, the easier it would be for you to identify whether you tend to ruminate or avoid the problematic thoughts, emotions, and sensations in your mind.

IT IS important to remind yourself that you should not associate your whole being with your low mood, but instead see it as a moment in your life that will fade away in its own time.

WHILE THIS CHAPTER focused on reducing depression by using mindfulness as part of a depression management plan, in the next chapter the focus will be on increasing happiness through mindfulness.

Mindfulness exercise

SELF COMPASSION

IF YOU HAVE issues you are going over in your head, you are stressed, anxious and being self-critical think about what you would say to a friend if they came to you saying the same things.

THINK about the negative self-talk or doubts you are telling yourself as though a friend was saying it to you and then respond how you would respond to a friend.

.   .   .

PRACTICE TREATING YOURSELF AS A FRIEND, reassuring yourself and being positive as you would to a friend.

PRACTICE FORGIVING yourself if you've made a mistake and practice loving yourself instead of directing negative and doubts on yourself.

NOTE: Mindfulness therapy is used in addition to traditional treatments and is generally used as ongoing management of emotions and feelings. This is not a replacement for any other treatment and if you are experiencing any symptoms of depression or addiction then consulting doctors and health care professionals would be the first step in getting treatment.

8

MINDFULNESS TO INCREASE HAPPINESS

"There's only one reason why you're not experiencing bliss at this present moment, and it's because you're thinking or focusing on what you don't have.... But, right now you have everything you need to be in bliss." - Anthony de Mello

Some say happiness is a choice, while others let their fates decide. Be that as it may, how you define happiness is entirely up to you. Regardless of how you experience or pursue it, when you know you are happy you tend to become more creative, positive, healthy, friendly, and even intelligent. Without a doubt, the feeling of happiness is what makes life worthwhile.

There are many ways towards experiencing happiness each day, but the key to all of them is mindfulness. Through mindfulness, you learn to let go of the things you cannot control, to appreciate what you have in the present moment, to perceive any situation in a curious and positive way, and to value yourself and your relationships with others. While it is inevitable that we go through good and bad experiences in life, mindfulness is what helps us develop the right attitude towards them.

Now you might be eager to learn about the different mindfulness techniques you can apply to increase your happiness. Well, here are some of the easiest ones that you can practice right now:

Smiling mindfulness

When someone smiles at you, it is almost instinctive for you to smile back, right? Even the act of smiling itself already causes you to feel lighter even just by a little bit.

Being mindful of this and the simple act of smiling at people you encounter will have a positive impact on your day and on others around you.

Go ahead and give it a try.

Breathing mindfulness

Smiling can also be incorporated into mindfulness meditation, as what mindfulness teacher and monk Thich Nhat Hanh once taught to his students. He calls it the Breathing and Smiling Meditation. Try meditating with the following lines inspired by the teacher himself to give this exercise a try:

As I breathe in, my mind becomes calm.

As I breathe out, my mind becomes clear.

As I breathe in, my body becomes relaxed.

As I breathe out, the tension is released.

Breathing in, I feel the air cleansing me.

Breathing out, I feel sadness leaving me.

Breathing in, I invite happiness and warmth.

Breathing out, I smile and feel gladness.

Breathing in, I invite light and love.

Breathing out, I smile and feel gratefulness.

Continue to breathe in, enjoying the sensation, and then breathing out and smiling. Notice how the smile relaxes your facial muscles and releases the tension from your mind and body. Keep practicing this meditation until you feel lighter and happier.

Mindfully Draw Mandalas

If you have ever experienced being deeply focused while drawing seemingly random, circular geometric designs, then you have already drawn mandalas before. Mandalas are geometric designs that traditional Buddhists believe to be the symbols of the universe. Therefore, Buddhists draw mandalas as a form of meditation to help gain balance and peace and to allow them to enter into a deeper state of mindfulness.

You can use a simple sheet of paper and any pen, crayon, watercolor, or whatnot to start drawing your mandalas. It does not have to look perfectly symmetrical because there is also beauty and wonder in asymmetry. To invoke feelings of happiness, you could even choose to draw using the colors that make you feel lighter and more cheerful.

Drawing mandalas allows you to be creative and free while focused at the same time. Best of all is that, as you notice the development of your own creation, you will feel increasingly satisfied, at peace, and happy. Once you have your finished product, you will be surprised to notice that the mandala is a reflection – if not an outlet – of what is going on in your mind.

Practice gratitude

There are numerous studies showing the benefits of gratitude on your happiness, a notable study in 2003 found that practicing gratitude daily leads to an increase in happiness, sense of well-being, better sleep and an ability to better deal with change.

People often react to the idea of daily gratitude by saying they have nothing to be grateful for on most days. However, you don't have to have significant life events occur to be grateful every day.

Many people in the world struggle without food, shelter or water and if they saw your life would believe it was their dream life. We often forget that having the basics to live is a reason to be grateful. You can be grateful that you have food, you have access to clean water, you have a roof over your head, your health, even small things such as being grateful that someone gave you a smile during the day or a song you liked was playing on the radio.

Being grateful for things that you have in your life - no matter how small they are or if you currently take them for granted - can help you see the abundance and joy you have in your life.

Practice being happy for other people's successes

Throughout history in all societies around the world, people have always been jealous of other people. Everybody experiences this at some time throughout their lives, whether a neighbour has bought a new car or someone at work has got a promotion, you may have felt jealous and annoyed at them.

The saying "keeping up with the Joneses" is a common example of people feeling that they constantly need to match other people's successes. They always purchase a new car if their neighbour has one or expensive material items just to impress other people.

"Too many people are buying things they can't afford, with money that they don't have... to impress people that they don't like!" - Will Smith

Practice being happy for other people's successes without feeling the need to match them or feeling jealous. Practicing gratitude about what you have will also help you feel happy and content.

Spend time in nature

Spending time in nature is a great way to practice mindfulness, this can be as simple as a walk in the park.

Studies have shown that spending time in nature has significant benefits such as:

- Decreases in stress levels
- Increases in happiness
- Your mind will feel more refreshed and calm
- Increased creativity
- Increases in energy and motivation

The list of benefits is much longer including health benefits, increases in self-esteem and help with depression, ADHD and anxiety treatments.

While you may feel you are too busy to spend time in nature, it's worth making the time even for a walk in the park on the weekend to see how it makes you feel. If you can make it a regular activity then you will likely notice all sorts of benefits to your health and life.

Play, have fun and disconnect

While being in nature has tremendous benefits, you don't have to spend time in nature to increase happiness and get similar health benefits. Having fun, enjoying the experience and disconnect from technology so you can be in the present moment will also benefit your body and mind.

Taking up a hobby or sport, spending time with you children or doing something creative like building something or painting is a form of mindfulness that also increases happiness.

If you have children, take time to play with them, go outside and play, build something with Lego, do a jigsaw puzzle, there are a range of activities you can do to play and increase happiness. Remember to be in the present moment when you do this, don't spend the time worrying about the future or past.

If you are in a relationship, organize a fun activity, disconnect from your phone and spend the time together being present in the moment and enjoying the experience.

A study at Cornell University found that experiences provide far more happiness than material possessions over time. We are happy when we first get a new item but that quickly fades; however, the happiness we get from experiences last and grows over time.

Experiences strengthen friendships, relationships and each time we look back at the experience we can relive the happiness and memories of the experience.

Even if there were difficult times or it didn't go as planned, we look back much more positively than when the event occurred. When something has gone wrong, we've probably heard someone say "this will make a funny story when we look back at it." This saying is very true - even experiences that seem bad at the time often make a funny story later that you can look back and enjoy.

The good times of experiences are strengthened in your memories and the bad times are reduced, making experiences, playtime and fun very valuable for happiness.

Everyday Mindfulness

Aside from these techniques, you can find happiness in whatever you do by simply savoring the moment itself. Allow your mind to be focused on what is happening in the present so that you will not miss the joy in it. Keep your senses, mind, and heart open and curious and you will see pleasure and joy in the simplest of experiences.

This book covers a lot of other techniques for mindfulness at work and everyday life day. In the next chapter, we'll look at other ways to experience mindfulness every day.

Mindfulness exercise

Practice gratitude

WRITE down 3 things you are grateful for. You can do this at the start of the day or at the end of the day, or even both if you want but it's important to write it down.

DOING it at the start of the day puts you in a positive mood for the morning, and doing it at the end of the day, helps calm your mind and give you thoughts to be grateful for before going to sleep.

NOBODY NEEDS to see this list, and they don't have to be big items. It might seem difficult at first but this list can just be anything: having a bed to sleep in, a roof over your head, running water, your health, your family, friends, a nice warm cup of coffee on a cold day. These are all reasons to be grateful.

ONCE YOU START PRACTICING GRATITUDE, you'll notice yourself appreciating more things throughout the day.

9

MINDFULNESS IN EVERYDAY LIFE

"The practice of mindfulness begins in the small, remote cave of your unconscious mind and blossoms with the sunlight of your conscious life, reaching far beyond the people and places you can see." - Earon Davis

MINDFULNESS IS SO simple you can practice it every day. The more you practice it, the more effortless it is to apply. Naturally, consistency is the key; so, if your goal is to become mindful in everyday life, then there are some things you can choose to do to build the habit.

You can discover for yourself the strategies that you can apply to become more mindful every day. However, to help you get started here are some simple yet effective yet techniques to practice being mindful regularly.

THIS IS a short summary as many of these techniques are covered in greater detail throughout this book.

.   .   .

SCHEDULE A DAILY "SILENT TIME"

THE MODERN WORLD is a noisy place, most especially if you are constantly connected to the internet and social media. Every day, we are bombarded with information, from work-related e-mails, telephone calls, and business meetings to photos, videos, and texts on social media.

IN THE MIDST of all this, it helps to set aside even just ten minutes of each waking day to be in complete silence. It is this "silent time" when you can turn off the digital devices, go to a quiet, private space, and then connect with yourself in that moment.

DURING THIS TIME, you can sit and meditate, practice yoga, or simply enjoy the feeling of your breath coming in and out of your body, as strange as that might sound. However, you spend this "silent time," let it be an opportunity for you to enjoy feeling alive without being influenced by anyone or anything else.

TO MAKE sure that you will not forget your "silent time," set a fixed schedule on when to do it. Then, set a daily alarm for it on your mobile phone. You can even post a note as a reminder on your mirror or refrigerator. For instance, if you prefer your silent time right before bedtime, then what you should do upon hearing the alarm is to set your phone on airplane mode or switch it off, and then begin. It is that simple.

CONNECT WITH NATURE

. . .

ON MOST DAYS, we are usually surrounded by man-made structures all the time. While there is nothing wrong with living in our own creations, we should always find the time to connect with the natural world. Mindfully walking in nature is scientifically proven to help reduce rumination and thus lower one's risk of developing depression.

A 2015 STUDY published in *Proceedings of the National Academy of Scientists* revealed that the participants who were asked to take a walk through nature – specifically grasslands with some surrounding shrubs and trees – revealed a decrease in rumination while those who walked through the cityscapes did not.

YOU DO NOT HAVE to travel far to connect with and be mindful of nature, although it is a good idea to go camping or to the beach every once in a while. On a daily basis, find the time to take the more nature-filled path to or from work, or spend your "silent time" in a park.

YOU CAN ALSO GROW a miniature garden at home and spend a few minutes each day taking care of your plants. Soon enough, you will notice that the restorative effects of nature are not only free, but also highly effective.

PRACTICE GRATITUDE

WHILE MOST OF us often remember our manners, and say "thank you", there are times when we become passive towards the things that we have, because we get too caught up chasing after the ones we do not. Therefore, it helps to pay more attention to our present moment and what we already have in it to feel more balanced and at peace with ourselves.

ONE OF THE easiest ways to nurture gratitude each day is by spending a few minutes before bed to remind ourselves of at least three things that we are grateful for. They do not have to be special and there is certainly no prerequisite to them in that you must feel ecstatic towards them.

IT CAN BE AS simple as having a warm bed in which to spend the night, the absence of pain from your body, or the good friends you get to share laughs with. When you end your day with good and grateful thoughts, you are more likely able to have a good night's rest as well.

MINDFUL LISTENING

WE'VE all encountered times where someone has been talking and we've "tuned out" as our mind wandered to other thoughts. They may not have noticed or it could have been more serious; for example, if you were in an important meeting and were then asked a question that you couldn't answer because you weren't listening.

NOT LISTENING CAN BE PERCEIVED as rudeness. It could make you appear uninterested or unintelligent or lazy if you are asked to respond and can't think of an answer that makes sense because you were occupied by your thoughts.

WHEN YOU ARE in a meeting or talking to people, practice mindful listening: listen to each word and sentence, ask them questions that apply to what they have said and don't think of other things while you are talking to them. If your mind wanders, snap it back to the conversation quickly and don't chase your thoughts or dwell on them.

MINDFUL WORKING

MANY PEOPLE LOOK to mindfulness to reduce stress and anxiety because they feel overwhelmed at work. You may experience the feeling that you are working all the time but never feel you are getting anything done.

YOU MAY FEEL CONSTANTLY BUSY, always running around, answering emails and phone calls, trying to keep your head above working and never getting to the important tasks or having any time to yourself.

MINDFULNESS AT WORK helps you take a step back, gain some calm and space and work on key tasks with focus and concentration, allowing you to work on what is important, instead of always feeling busy and overwhelmed.

THERE IS a chapter that covers mindfulness at work in much greater detail in this book along with a range of practical techniques.

PRACTICE RESISTING distractions

. . .

WE ARE CONSTANTLY BOMBARDED by distractions these days, from emails, messages, smart phone notifications and all ranges of electronics devices.

THIS IMPACTS OUR WORK, our personal time, relationships and all areas of our life. Our concentration span is lower and we are unable to focus on anything for long periods of time.

TURN OFF NOTIFICATIONS FOR APPS, practice turning off your smartphone when you are having a conversation with someone, close your email and put your phone away when you are concentrating on a task at work.

YOU CAN USE a timer to see how long you can focus on one task without switching to another task or distraction such as Facebook etc. Practice being more present with less distractions and work on increasing the time you focus for set periods of time.

MINDFULNESS IN RELATIONSHIPS

RELATIONSHIPS TAKE WORK, often when we have been in a relationship for a while, we fall into routines and habits without being mindful of the other person. You may have found in past relationships you were shocked or surprised that the other person was unhappy in a relationship, or you may have found yourself unhappy that they took you for granted.

COMMON ISSUES in relationships is feeling the other person is not listening to you: they are occupied with their computer or TV when you are around; they don't take the time to have deep conversations with you; they are unaware of your needs or how they can help you.

YOU MAY HAVE HAD a partner tell you that you don't listen to them or are never fully there or that you do not pay attention to them.

BEING mindful in a relationship means being fully present with the other person. Mindful listening is a good place to start. When you are with your partner turn off the TV or other distractions, have a conversation with them, go for a walk and talk, explore nature or a park or an activity where you are both present enjoying the experience and each other's company.

MINDFULNESS IN RELATIONSHIPS is covered in greater detail later in this book.

MINDFULNESS WHEN EATING and drinking

YOU CAN PRACTICE mindfulness when eating and drinking. Don't just pick any food and eat it quickly. Be mindful of the food you are eating: carefully select the food; look at it to notice the texture and details; notice the smell of the food; eat slowly and savor the taste of it.

YOU CAN DO the same with drinking. Be mindful of the process of preparing your tea or coffee and take time to relax during the preparation of it. If you are drinking a cold drink, examine small details such as the moisture on the glass. Drink slowly, enjoy the taste and how refreshing it is.

. . .

WITH MINDFUL DRINKING AND EATING, you are mindful of what you are eating and the joy of eating or drinking, savoring and enjoying the flavors and texture.

WALKING mindfulness

WALKING IS a great way to relax, unwind and calm the mind, it can also be a form of mindfulness and meditation.

IF YOU ARE FEELING stressed or are stuck on a problem or task and can't make any progress, go for a short walk to take your mind off things. When you are being mindful, don't have earphones in but focus instead on the sounds and sights around you. Notice the sounds. Pay attention to your surroundings: notice how it feels to move; the feeling of your feet on the ground; the sun on your body or wind on your face.

WHEN YOU WALK, be present and don't distract yourself with music or thoughts of the past or future, just enjoy the experience of walking in that moment.

THE POINT of walking mindfully is not to come up with a solution to a problem or de-stress. The purpose should be just to enjoy the walk. You will often find that taking your mind off your worries and issues will help you approach them from a calmer perspective allowing you to better deal with them.

. . .

Mindfulness with bad habits

IF YOU ARE smoker or have a bad habit, you can be mindful of the bad effects of the habit. With smoking, you may feel a craving for a cigarette, you may then feel satisfied when you smoke; however. you are not being mindful of smoking.

NOTICE why you are feeling the craving to smoke. Is it because you are stressed? Do you need a break from work? What is going on at the time when you feel that craving?

WHEN YOU HAVE A SMOKE, are there other people around? Are you talking to people? Could the feeling of satisfaction be from having a break from work when it is stressful and talking to people about the issues or distraction?

WHEN YOU SMOKE BE mindful of the taste - that you are inhaling poisonous smoke into your body, the taste of burning ash - and notice how it makes your breath and clothes smell.

BEING mindful of your bad habits along with the impact they have on you can help you move away from doing them on autopilot. You become mindful of the craving when you feel it, along with other possible causes. You are then mindful of the relief you get from the bad habit and what else could be causing that relief along with being more aware of the negative effects of the habit.

NOTE: Smoking is a serious health issue and is difficult to stop. If you wish to stop smoking you should consult a doctor or experts to help with quitting. This is not a recommendation to only use mindfulness when quitting smoking, it is a technique that can be used in addition to other treatments, not a replacement.

MEDITATION

MEDITATION AND MINDFULNESS ARE DIFFERENT; however, a daily meditation habit can have a huge impact in helping you be more mindful throughout the day.

MEDITATION CAN BE DONE for only a few minutes each day, it takes practice to meditate correctly but over time there will be very noticeable effects on your mood and mindset providing you with more calm during the day.

YOU CAN START with a guided meditation session for a few minutes. Meditation with a specific focus on mindfulness and resources is covered in more detail throughout this book.

PAUSE AND TAKE a deep breath during the day

THROUGHOUT THE DAY, you may find yourself stressed and overwhelmed. Whenever this happens, just pause for a moment, take a deep breath in and a long slow breath out. Do this for a few breaths until you feel a bit calmer.

TAKING EVEN a few seconds throughout the day to pause and have a deep breath and focus only on the breath can bring enough calm into that moment to help you relax and stop the stress from escalating further.

Bring yourself back to the present moment, focus on what you need to do at that time and don't worry about the past or future.

As you can see, it is not so hard to find the time to be mindful in everyday life. None of the exercises take more than a few minutes of your time. However, by practicing them each day, their nurturing effect on you will last throughout the rest of your life.

Mindfulness Exercise

Pause and take a few seconds before leaving home, work or car

This is a simple technique but has a lot of value (it is covered in more detail in this book).

You may find you often forget things especially when in a hurry. When you forget things, this can impact your entire day. This could be causing you to run late, locking you out of your car, being unable to complete your work or having to go back to get the item you forgot.

You may have also found that you can't remember whether you turned off the iron or heater or locked the door which causes you stress during the day and you should contact someone to check or go back to make sure.

.   .   .

BEFORE YOU LEAVE YOUR HOME, work or car, pause for a moment - pause and take a deep breath, be present - check you have everything you need and aren't leaving without forgetting anything.

BEFORE LEAVING THE HOUSE, you may want to check the oven, the iron, that you have your keys, that you have locked the door correctly etc.

THIS SHORT TECHNIQUE will do wonders to help calm your mind. It will help ensure you don't forget items along with actions such as turning things off and locking doors.

AFTER CHECKING ITEMS, pause for a few seconds and take a deep breath before leaving.

10

MINDFULNESS IN RELATIONSHIPS

"The most precious gift we can offer others is our presence. When mindfulness embraces those we love, they will bloom like flowers." - Thich Nhat Hanh

Mindfulness is an essential component in establishing healthy relationships with ourselves and with others. It helps us become more compassionate, kind, grateful, forgiving, and understanding. It enables us to clearly see our own intentions and those of others in the relationship. It keeps us from being too critical and perfectionist because it allows us to acknowledge both the positive and negative aspects of a relationship.

You may have experienced times when someone was talking and your mind wandered and you didn't hear what they were saying because you were focused on your thoughts instead. It's possible they noticed this as well, and told you that weren't listening to them, or perhaps you were unable to continue the conversation or ask them questions and the conversation ended on a bad note.

There may have been times where you were around a friend or loved one but instead of spending quality time with them, you were watching TV, checking email, looking at Facebook, checking your phone or other tasks and you weren't giving them your full attention.

Mindfulness can teach you to be more present when you are around people, giving people your full attention: both showing that to them and giving them your mental attention to focus on what they are saying and listening to them. This will, in time, dramatically improve your interactions with people, your relationships with them, how they perceive you and the quality of your life.

To help you use mindfulness in enhancing the quality of your relationships, here are some of its practical strategies you can apply:

Listen mindfully when the other person is talking

Most people tend to listen to their loved ones and at the same time try to construct responses in their mind. Then they would wait for the other person to finish speaking so that they can share their own message. Another common thing is when people only "half listen" to the other person because their mind gets caught up in their other thoughts. Unfortunately, bad habits are often the cause of conflict behind many relationship troubles.

If you have caught yourself committing either of these two, or something other than listening intently and wholeheartedly, then now is the opportunity for you to enhance your mindful listening ability.

Mindful listening is one of the foundational elements on which a strong relationship is built. This is the type of listening wherein you listen to the message that the other person is sharing with you without any judgment whatsoever. This is only possible when you let go of any opinions, ideas, and other thoughts that cross your mind as you listen to that person.

Now this is easier said than done, but through constant practice you will gradually find yourself listening more to the other person than to your own thoughts.

Here are some tips on how to help you become a mindful listener:

- When the other person invites you to listen, stop moving or doing anything else and engage your eyes and ears towards that person.
- If you are listening in person, maintain natural eye contact

so that you can also see their facial expressions and overall body language while they are speaking.

- Bring your entire focus towards that person's message. Ask questions to deepen your understanding and make the appropriate responses to keep you grounded on the message (such as by saying, "I see...", "uh huh..." or whatever else is natural to you).
- When thoughts unrelated to the message pop into your mind, draw your focus back toward what the person is saying. You can ask questions to clarify and retain your focus as well.
- If your mind wanders a lot you can focus on the words they are saying by focusing on each word and sentence after they say it in your mind. By changing your thoughts from your own mind to repeating what they are saying in your mind and focusing on this, you can calm your mind and stop it wandering onto other thoughts when someone is talking to you.
- Nurture an attitude of curiosity and acceptance as you listen to that person. Let go of the temptation to give the person an answer or to solve that person's problem when he/she is only asking for you to listen.

The next time your loved one is sharing their thoughts with you, just relax, be mentally immersed, and listen without the urge to comment.

Enjoy the present moment with each other

The art of mindfulness teaches an essential lesson, and it is the fact that nothing is ever permanent. For instance, all human relationships end in their own time - such as best friends growing apart, a loved one passing away, or lovers going through a breakup. We must, therefore, make the most of the present moment by being completely engaged in it.

To make each moment meaningful with your loved ones, remember the following mindfulness tips:

- Block out your special time with that person. This means you should not allow anything else, even work, to distract you while you are spending time with them. Those moments should be treated as the most important appointments in your agenda.
- Put away the smartphones or anything that could distract you from focusing fully on that person. Ask the other person to do the same so that you two can really get to be fully present in the moment.
- Do something meaningful with that other person. You could enjoy communing with nature together, for instance. Allow your creativity to take you to places without having to spend much.
- Organize an experience or activity together. If you are unsure what to talk about or the weather conditions aren't good for nature or the outdoors, do an activity that you can share and enjoy together. Take a pottery workshop, attend a dance class, go ice skating etc. There are a range of activities where you can spend time together, enjoying the moment and time together that you can talk and laugh about later and will strengthen your relationship.
- Have a real conversation with each other, if you find conversation hard or are unsure what to speak about, you can prepare some questions to ask each other to get to know each other better. There are countless questions online to get to know people better: you can look these up before hand, write them down or print some so you don't forget and make the effort to have a genuine conversation to get to know each other better.

Take this moment as an opportunity for you to know who the important people are in your life. Find opportunities to mindfully spend time with them, to get to know them and to just enjoy the pleasure of being alive and sharing a relationship with them. Then, during those times, avoid getting distracted from that person's company and instead cherish being with them.

Be mindful of your response to others

Many relationships fail because people are too quick to react and do not have the patience to step back and be more mindful of how they communicate their thoughts. If you have had encountered issues in your past relationships and interactions with others because you forget to think before you speak, then mindfulness can help you exercise patience to respond rather than react.

How do you become more mindful in communicating with your loved ones?

Here are the tips that can help you out:

- Each day, nurture an attitude of patience and mindfulness. Listen to your thoughts that might be too critical or judgmental towards the other person and see if you can transform them into curiosity and patience.
- Notice the times when you tend to lose your cool too quickly while spending time with the other person. Try to understand why you usually react too quickly, then figure out how you can overcome challenges that keep you from thinking before speaking.
- Let go of expectations or assumptions regarding the other person. Often, we become frustrated when what we expect to happen does not actually transpire. It is important to remember that there is no certain thing in life except the present moment, so one must foster hope rather than expectations.
- Practice starting your responses with "I feel..." or "I think..." instead of "you should." This way of communicating your thoughts is less demanding of the other person and more honest and open about how you really do feel about the situation.

It takes effort to hold yourself back from reacting immediately when you are communicating with others, especially with people you have gotten used to being with. However, the more you exercise mindfulness as you interact with them, the better you will be at stopping to think first before you respond.

As you can see, mindfulness not only benefits yourself mentally and physically but your social relationships as well.

Nurture your relationship with yourself

While mindfulness when interacting with others is very important, you should also remember that mindfulness can help establish a better relationship with yourself. Continue to practice the mindfulness techniques in this book and you will learn to become more loving and caring towards yourself, to move from self-criticism towards self-improvement, and to be grateful for being who you are.

Mindfulness Exercise
Listen to other people mindfully

MINDFUL LISTENING IS one of the most important skills you can develop in relationships and when dealing other people.

Practice mindful listening over the next few days whenever possible.

IF YOU ARE HAVING dinner with your partner or a friend, turn your phone off and practice talking to them and having a conversation without checking your phone or being distracted by notifications.

FOCUS on what they are saying and don't be distracted by other thoughts or ideas. Be present and listen to what they are saying.

PLAN AN ACTIVITY with your friend or partner. This could be something as simple as going for a walk. Put your phone away and spend time with them, fully immerse yourself in the activity and your time with them.

IN THE WORKPLACE or anywhere during your day, practice talking to someone without distraction, listen to what they are saying and if your mind wanders practice bringing it back. Focus on each word they are saying and bring focus back to that if your mind wanders.

IF YOU ARE in a meeting with people, turn your phone off, concentrate on what the person that is speaking is saying. Bring a pen and paper, make notes of any key points and anything you want to say later, don't hold them in your mind or be distracted by your thoughts.

11

PRACTICAL MINDFULNESS TECHNIQUES FOR WORK

"*This is the real secret of life — to be completely engaged with what you are doing in the here and now. And instead of calling it work, realize it is play.*" - Alan Watts

People not familiar will generally not associate it with work or productivity; however, mindfulness is undoubtedly one of the most powerful tools you can use to be productive and creative at work.

Mindfulness is awareness. While work will take up a large part of your day and life we are often on auto-pilot, not being aware of what causes us stress or what we should be working on.

Being mindful at work involves being more aware of our life, the factors surrounding our work and what we are working on.

Mindfulness can be awareness of what causes us stress or problems and addressing them or awareness of what we are working on e.g. selecting the task to focus on for a set amount of time without distractions.

Mindfulness allows you to be less reactive with what you work on. It is the active choice of what to work on instead of reactive choice, combined with the ability to focus for longer periods of times that make mindfulness such a huge benefit to work and productivity.

Mindfulness increases your ability to produce a higher quality of work and you will feel more engaged in the task, so it's likely you will enjoy tasks that currently seem like chores.

There are several techniques you can apply to apply mindfulness at work. Starting your day with mindfulness meditation is helpful, however having your day planned and being more active rather that reactive will mean you are less likely to be overcome by the hustle and bustle that will greet you at the office.

We'll go through a range of techniques and methods by which mindfulness can benefit you at work. Some of these techniques are not purely mindfulness techniques but they address the causes of why people struggle to incorporate mindfulness into their day.

Become fully aware of your goals and work role

It might sound silly to even suggest this, but the truth is that some people tend to forget how important their role is in a company or business. For instance, have you ever experienced walking into the office without feeling "present" at work? It is either that your mind is elsewhere or that you feel unmotivated even before you had begun your day.

You go into the office, answer emails, sit in meetings and finish the day and feel stressed that you didn't get anything done. You can't remember what you did the day before because you're just in a rut, mindlessly reacting to busy work as it appears throughout the day.

You can break out of your mental work "rut" by immersing yourself in the present moment while at work. The first and easiest thing to do would be to quickly review your job description, your KPIs and yearly targets. This will instantly give you a sense of what your role is as you can break this down into monthly and weekly goals and then establish your purpose for going to work that day.

You can also start each work week (or even every work day) by answering questions such as, "Where am I? Why am I here? What are my targets? What am I working towards? What needs to be done today? What is going on right now? What do I think and how do I feel about all these?"

After answering these questions, you would then be able to proactively choose to be mentally – not just physically – present at work. Thus, you would become more in tune with your role inside the workplace, in that you can avoid doing the job absentmindedly now that you have a clearer picture of what your role is, what your goals are and how to get there.

Choose your number one priority

"Busy" should never be synonymous with "productive," because you could be busy doing a handful of unproductive tasks, but you could never be unproductive when you are focused on a single but highly important task. By the end of the day, the "productive" person will be one step closer to their goal while the "busy" one would have just spread themselves thin without really accomplishing anything.

How do you use mindfulness to become more productive and less "busy?" The answer is simple: highlight your number one priority. To do that, you must first know what your goal is at work. Is there a project that you need to accomplish within a specific time frame? If so, flesh out the goal in the most detailed way possible. You can use SMART (Specific, Measurable, Achievable, Relevant, and Timely) goal-setting strategy by George T. Doran to clearly define your work goal.

After you have fleshed out your goal, your next step is to delineate the objectives or sub-goals you need to accomplish to reach that goal successfully. The SMART goal-setting strategy can help you to do that as well.

Once you have your main goal and objectives, you should then break the objectives down into daily tasks, keeping in mind that certain tasks need to be accomplished before you can move on to the next. It is also important to take into consideration how you can delegate certain tasks to other people and whether certain tasks really are necessary or not. Through mindful planning, you can select what it is exactly that you need to work on.

After you have successfully divided your objectives into daily tasks, you can then see quite clearly what your number one priority is for each day. That priority should be the only thing you should focus on to accomplish your main goal. It goes without saying as well that you need to say "no" to tasks that are unrelated to that work priority. Otherwise, your main goal will be compromised.

Plan your day the night before

A lot of stress and anxiety with work comes from feeling constantly behind on the day.

Below is a common scenario for many people that you, unfortunately, may be all too familiar with:

You wake up to your alarm clock (after hitting the snooze button several times, feeling tired and needing coffee. You rush to get ready for work, have a coffee, shower then run out the door to the train. You can't get on the train as it's so busy, then you find a train is delayed or cancelled. If you drive, you find that you are stuck in peak hour traffic and feel stressed and angry. You finally make it to work late, open your emails and find 100 unanswered emails that you hurry to answer before rushing to a meeting you are unprepared for.

You are behind all day, reacting to work, feeling stressed then end the day feeling you got nothing done. This happens day after day, week after week and eventually years.

It doesn't have to be this way. By using mindfulness, you can completely change your mindset, mood and life with simple changes.

The first change is to plan your day the night before. Doing what is listed below will make a massive difference to the start of your day:

- Put your clothes out for the next day
- Schedule your day in your calendar
- Schedule your most important task in your calendar
- Prepare/plan your breakfast and lunch
- Prepare all documents and bag for the next day

Anything you can do the night before for the next day will save a huge amount of time and stress the next morning.

In the evening, think about your usual morning routine, what you need for the next day and if there is anything you can prepare for the night before.

Wake up early and enjoy calm at the start of the day

We probably all know the sayings about waking up early such as:

- "the early bird gets the worm" and
- "early to bed, early to rise, makes you healthy, wealthy and wise."

Yet most of us struggle to wake up early and tell ourselves things like:

- "I'm not a morning person"
- "I'll never be a morning person"
- "I can't wake up early"
- "I always hit the snooze button until the last minute to wake up"
- "I need those extra few mins in the morning"

You may have tried to wake up early, been unable to sustain it, find it too difficult or you may find you already wake up early enough.

However, if you are feeling rushed and stressed in the day, then waking up even a few minutes earlier can make a big difference.

By the end of the day your mental energy is exhausted and you just feel like sitting in front of TV and find anything that involves thinking too difficult.

However, if you wake up earlier and are calmer and prepared in the morning, you will find the rest of the day flows smoother.

While morning routines and getting up earlier is an in-depth topic for another book, you can start with simple practices that take little changes or effort to your daily routine to sleeping patterns.

Waking up even 15 minutes earlier, followed by spending 5 to 10 minutes meditating and having calm at the start of the day is a practice many successful people believe has been a contributing factor to their success.

Be mindful of what you eat and drink in the morning

There is a chapter on mindful eating and drinking which goes into detail on this but what you eat and drink has an impact on your mind and body.

When we wake up in the morning, we feel tired and we often assume we need coffee; however, a lot of tiredness in the morning is caused by dehydration.

Keeping a bottle of water next to your bed and having a big drink of water after waking up will do wonders for making you feel less tired and more refreshed in the morning.

You can be mindful of what you eat and drink for breakfast and throughout the day. This is covered in more detail in other chapters but try staying hydrated by drinking water throughout the day, starting with first thing in the morning and notice how it affects your mood, energy levels and productivity.

Leave for work earlier than required

As mentioned previously, a common pattern of stress and anxiety is feeling rushed and behind on the day, which often occurs by getting off to a bad start to the day.

Leaving your house earlier than required will reduce the amount of stress in the morning.

Leaving earlier than required gives you a bit of a margin in the morning - you have more time if the trains are cancelled or delayed. You have more time if there is bad traffic or delays on the road.

Leaving for work earlier than required makes a big difference in being less stressed in the morning which will flow into the rest of your day.

Take a deep breath and take 10 seconds before leaving the house or car

How many times have you left for work or rushed out of the house only to realize you've forgotten something after you left? Have you ever locked your keys in the car or forgotten something in the car? Can you think of a recent time this has happened?

This occurs when our mind is distracted and we are occupied with thoughts, worrying about things in the future or dwelling on things from the past. You may notice you are more forgetful when you are more stressed or in a hurry.

Firstly, planning for the next day is important. Putting everything out the night before will help you be more prepared in the morning. You can just follow a routine: you could have a checklist near the door of everything you need to bring.

Secondly, a simple technique that helps with this is just taking time to pause before leaving the house. Take time at the front door to pause, take some deep breaths, check that you have everything you need for the day.

You can do this anytime you are leaving a place. This is also helpful when leaving a car as well. 10 seconds is not long at all but the time savings and additional sense of calm are significant over time.

This simple technique helps prevent you from having to go back to the house after leaving or having to go to work or elsewhere without being fully prepared and having all the things you need.

Use transit time wisely

The average transit time for most people is between 1 to 2 hours each day. We all have 24 hours in a day. If you take out 8 hours for sleep and 8 hours for work, you have only 8 hours remaining, so these 1 to 2 hours a day comprise a large amount of your free time.

We often waste this time, listening to bad radio ads in the car, not doing anything on the train.

You can change this to be productive time or time that helps you calm your mind.

Ideas on how to use your transit time better:

- **Listen to an audiobook** - You can do this in the car or on the train. It will allow you to get through an additional book a week with just the time you are in transit
- **Read a book** - not possible if you are driving but if you are on the train, use this time to switch off from phone and notifications and immerse yourself in the book
- **Learn a language** - many people say they want to learn a language but they don't have the time. Use this time to learn a language with tapes or apps
- **Write or keep a journal** - Writing takes practice but over

time becomes easier. It doesn't matter what you write about. Often you have a lot of thoughts racing around your head but once you start to write them out, it takes them out of your head and puts them on paper and you can reduce your stress and anxiety. Your thoughts race at a million miles an hour but you can only write at a certain speed so once you try to write down your thoughts or journal, your thoughts become more structured and clear. It can be good to do this on the way home, so when you get home you don't dwell on issues more or bring them up with your partner and spend the evening complaining about work.

- **Meditate** - You can't do this while driving but you can listen to guided meditation, even if you are standing, to bring some calm into your day and meditate during the transit time on the train to work.

When getting started with mindfulness and meditation, you may find you are still too stressed during a lot of the day. It takes time to calm your mind and get into a routine. You can work on tasks that are important to you during your transit time that will save you time in the morning or the next day but be mindful of how you work on them.

Again, as mentioned several times, often you may feel productive but you're busy, switching between tasks and checking notifications. If you are going to use transit time to work on tasks, turn off notifications and distractions and don't listen to music with lyrics or audiobooks while trying to do another task.

Focus fully on the task at hand and immerse yourself in it. When you find your mind wandering, bring your attention back to the task. If you feel the need to check Facebook or emails, notice that urge, acknowledge it and let the urge go, then bring your focus back to the task you should be focusing on.

Do the most important tasks first

Once you have arrived at work, you should have already planned your most important task to work on.

Most emails are not urgent or important, often we fall into the trap of getting caught up with busy work by responding to emails first and then we never get time for the most important work.

This is a factor for a continuous cycle where we never get ahead of the work we need to be working on.

Start your day by working on the most important tasks before getting to emails and busy work.

If at the start, you feel you can't work on the most important tasks before checking emails, try coming into work a bit earlier and have 15 to 30 mins where you work on important tasks, knowing that is bonus time in your day and that you don't need to feel stressed by not checking emails or responding to phone calls straight away.

Focus on one task at a time

Multitasking is the perceived ability to do multiple tasks at the same time or rapidly switching from one task to another. It might seem as if multitasking will enable you to accomplish more things within the day.

However, multitasking is a myth. It's not possible for most people to do multiple things at the same time. If you are switching between tasks rapidly, you may feel productive as you are stimulating lots of brain activity, but that brain activity is stimulated by feeling busy and stressed not by producing quality results or output.

When you multitask, you are switching between tasks without ever giving your full focus to them. Along with not fully concentrating on a task, there is a switching cost, where you lose productivity and focus switching between tasks.

While multi-tasking might make you feel like you're busy and getting things done, the truth is that you can actually produce significantly better quality output when you select only one task to focus on for a set period of time before you move on to the next one. Doing this also makes you feel less stressed, more fulfilled and effective at what you do.

In short, multitasking might cause you to "feel" more productive, but the result is actually the opposite.

Mindfulness helps you focus better and increase the amount of time you can focus on one particular task. One of the best strategies to compel yourself to single-task instead of multi-task is by creating a daily agenda, scheduling in tasks with timeframes.

Select one most important item for the day and schedule it in to work on first thing in the morning, if possible. Block the time out in your calendar like a meeting, you can select two to four other items for the day and schedule these in as well.

By creating a single flow of everything that needs to be done during that day, you will be more guided on which task to focus on first before you move on to the next one. It is also a good idea – although not always necessary – to set a timer right before you start the task. That way, you will become fully aware of the time limit you have for that task and so would be less likely to break away from your concentration.

During that time make sure you remove distractions:

- Close your email and don't check it. Set an auto-reply saying you'll be available later in the day
- Turn off notifications that may distract you
- Put your phone away
- Let calls go to an answering machine
- Do not connect to the internet if possible - you can do research before starting the task so you don't need to connect to the internet
- Have a notepad and pen nearby to write any thoughts or reminders to go back to them later
- Put headphones in with classical music or other music without lyrics
- Let people know not to disturb you in a polite way or with a sign on your desk
- Let them know when you'll be available again so they know when they can contact you or you'll get back to them

Select the task you will be working on. Be mindful of the task, why you are doing it and how you feel before starting it. Notice any resistance to starting the task and why you feel that way. Commit to focusing on that task for the set period of time you have allocated and then start the task.

When your mind wanders, remember why you are doing this task, notice the distraction and your mind, make a note of anything in a notepad and then bring your focus back to the task.

This is a lot more difficult than it seems. You will find at the start you will want to get up from your desk, check your phone; you will think of other things you need to do and feel the urge to do them at that moment. It takes practice but over time you will find you continuously improve and will get more done with less stress.

Condition yourself to enter the state of flow

Another key to being mindful when working is entering a "state of flow," which is a special mental state in which highly mindful individuals find themselves when they are a hundred percent focused, involved, and passionate about the process of the task they have at hand.

In short, when you are in this state, you are completely absorbed in what you are doing, so much so that you no longer care about the irrelevant happenings in your surroundings or even the time.

The term "flow" used in this concept was coined by Hungarian psychologist Mihaly Csikszentmihalyi. According to him, there are six defining factors that will let you know you have entered the state of flow:

First, you become intensely focused on the present moment.

Second, you can combine awareness with action.

Third, you no longer feel self-conscious or entertain self-conscious thoughts (am I doing a good job? What will they think of my work?); fourth, you will feel a sense of complete personal control over the task, or in other words, you feel a sense of ownership to the activity.

Fifth, your subjective perspective of time is changed in that you no longer notice how fast or slow time passes you by as you work.

Sixth, you feel pure joy from doing the task, so much so that you do not even think about the reward you would get after completing the task because the task in and of itself is already rewarding to you.

With all these in mind, you might now be eager to enter this state whenever you have a task you need to accomplish. But how do you set the right conditions? Csikszentmihalyi said that three conditions need to be met to enter this state.

It is highly important to remind yourself of these conditions before you start your work (or any other activity, for that matter) because these will enable you to become effortlessly mindful. Here are the three conditions:

· You must have clearly defined goals and a means of tracking your progress. This condition serves as the foundation of your activity and will enable you to see clearly the direction you need to take.

· You must have access to immediate and clear feedback. This will aid you in making the necessary adjustments to how you approach the task while you are in the state of flow.

· Your perceived skills (or the skills and talents you think you have) should be in line with the perceived challenges of the task (or the difficulty of what you need to do to work on and accomplish the task). It is important to be confident in your ability to work on and successfully finish the task to maintain the state of flow.

Once these conditions are met, you can easily enter and maintain the state of flow while at work.

Overcome Hindrances to Mindful Working

Entering the state of flow is easier for some than others, it takes practice of focused work and mindfulness. In his book, Csikszentmihalyi highlights three of the main hindrances that keep one from being able to work mindfully, and they are Boredom, Anxiety, and Indifference. We have all been through them, so it is safe to assume that you are quite familiar with them yourself. Let us look at each of them and what you can do to overcome them.

Boredom keeps you from entering the state of flow because you perceive the task as too easy in comparison with your skill set. To overcome boredom and become focused and intrinsically motivated to work, here are the strategies you can apply:

· Follow a motivational weekday morning routine.

Whatever your line of work is, it is always best to start the day right so that you will have the right attitude the moment you get to work. Think of the factors that cause you to come to work feeling bored and then do something about them. For example, if the traffic to work wears you out, you can listen to a motivational audiobook while in transit.

· Make your workspace look inspirational.

Is the mere look of your office boring? If so, then no wonder you feel bored while at work! It is time to change things up by using office supplies that make you want to work. In fact, improving your work space does not have to cost much. A quick search online for free tips on how to make it look less boring and more inspiring is all you need to do to get started.

· Ask for more responsibilities or a promotion.

The good thing about having a work that is "too easy" is that it becomes quite effortless for you to overachieve in it. Do that and then document everything you do so that you can have the courage to ask for added responsibilities (and of course, better pay) later.

Anxiety is the opposite of boredom, and it is a hindrance from you being able to work mindfully because you think that the task is too difficult for you. Thankfully, you can employ the following techniques to successfully overcome anxiety and enter the state of flow:

• Become highly organized.

When tasks start to pile up and become overwhelming, the last thing you want is for them to be disorganized. If you are starting to feel anxious about the work ahead, then channel your energy towards organizing everything. Clear everything out and then focus only on the things you need to work on your top one priority.

• Know your limits and set them straight.

If you know for a fact that a task being handed out to you is too difficult, do not be afraid to ask for your superior's advice. Let them know about your limits and how you can ask for help. It is better for them to know than for you to just say "yes" but then not deliver as expected.

- Enhance your skills.

What is it about the job that you find it too difficult? Take a step back and mindfully assess those aspects. Once you have identified them, you can then easily determine the steps you need to take to enhance your skills and become more qualified for it.

Finally, let us move on to the last, which is indifference. The reason why some are hindered by it is that both the challenge of the task and their skillsets are low, thus resulting in a general lack of interest. To gain genuine interest towards the task, you can apply the following strategies:

- Approach the task with curiosity.

The main ingredient that makes any job "bad" is a bad attitude. However, if your attitude towards the work is one that is constructive and curious, then the work itself becomes more interesting. Before you approach the task, avoid saying "I don't care about this anymore." Instead, adopt the mindset of an eager beginner saying, "I wonder if I do this instead of that…"

- Engage in a little friendly competition.

Beating the highest score always has an element of fun to it, regardless of what the task is. This will make you feel a lot less indifferent and a lot more engaged towards the task. In fact, a little competition will enable you to pay more attention to your performance each day. Keep in mind that you can compete with yourself as well, and not just with others.

For instance, you can try to beat your score from yesterday. Focus time is a good way to do this. See how long you can focus on a task without distraction, start with 5 minutes, then see if you can get to 10 minutes and eventually 30 minutes.

After you have reached 30 minutes of focused concentration, take a break and see how many 30 minute uninterrupted blocks you can do during each day.

- Plan a reward in relation to the task.

Sometimes, you become more immersed in the task when you have something to look forward to after its completion. For instance, you can plan a vacation and then focus on your work so that you can afford to take that trip. Create milestones in the task in relation to the reward so that you will continue to feel motivated to work as you see your progress.

Create a shutdown ritual

Often, we often find that in the evening or at night when we are having dinner with our family or trying to sleep we can't shut off our mind from thinking about work or things we need to do.

It's important to have a ritual where you shutdown from work for the day so your evening and night time is not spent with your mind still distracted by thoughts of the past or future.

At the end of the day, finish any emails you need to respond to. Look at any work you haven't finished for the day and schedule it in for the next day.

If required, put on an auto-reply, letting people know that you will respond to their email between certain hours the next day.

If you have work on your laptop or computer, save it, schedule it in for completion the next day and shut down all work windows and programs. Close all browser windows and fully shut down your computer.

You don't need to finish all your work, you just need to finish your work day without stressing or thinking about things you need to do still. Taking unfinished work and scheduling it for the next day will mean you know when you will work on it and then you can't think about it until that time.

You can plan your next day: put out clothes and prepare for the next day as part of your shutdown ritual.

This will help you enjoy your evenings with guilt free time where you are trying to enjoy an activity but feel guilty you didn't finish the work. It will help you get a better sleep without worrying about unfinished work or emails. You know when you will work on them and finish them the next day.

Mindfulness at work conclusion

If you find you still can't enjoy your job no matter how much effort you put into to being mindful, then your effort may be in the wrong job for you. You need to decide what is best for you and your life but if you decide to find another job, you can create a plan on how to go about it in a practical way. Take your time in making this decision and be utterly mindful about each step you take.

Now that you are well-acquainted with these mindfulness techniques for work, the only thing you need to do is to start putting them into practice. You have everything to gain by being more productive and less stressed and nothing to lose by applying mindfulness at work.

The moment you find yourself effortlessly slipping into the state of flow each time you are at work, you know that you are genuinely interested in what you do. You know what they say, "if you love what you do, then you will never have to work a day in your life."

Mindfulness takes practice and time, it is like going to the gym: it will be difficult at first and you won't see results and it will be easier to just sit on the couch, watch TV and eat junk food. However, over time, you will notice your muscles will stretch and grow slowly, you will find less resistance and you will enjoy going to the gym and exercising.

This is the same with mindfulness, concentration and focus. At the start your mind will continue to race and it will revert to checking social media and emails and finding small constant distractions. However, over time, your focus muscle will grow, you will be more aware of what you are working on and why; you will be mindful of distractions and work to minimize them. It takes time and practice but mindfulness has massive implications for reducing stress and increasing productivity which will lead to a happier, more successful and fulfilled life.

Mindfulness exercise

Focus on your most important task without distraction

PLAN the next day and set your most important task for tomorrow. Schedule in a time to do it and block that time off in your calendar like it is a meeting. Try to schedule it as early as possible in the day.

DURING THAT TIME turn off distractions and just focus on that task: don't check emails, phone notifications or the internet. If your task requires going on the internet, then close all other browser tabs and windows and just focus on that one.

DON'T LET your thoughts or mind wander but concentrate on the task at hand.

IF IT'S TOO big to finish that's ok, just start and work on it for a set period of time: you can try for just 15 minutes to start.

WORKING on your concentration will help build your attention muscle so you become better at focusing on one thing at a time and being more present and mindful.

12

MINDFULNESS MEDITATION

"*indfulness is the aware, balanced acceptance of the present experience. It isn't more complicated than that. It is opening to or receiving the present moment, pleasant or unpleasant, just as it is, without either clinging to it or rejecting it.*" - Sylvia Boorstein

WHEN YOU ENTER MINDFULNESS MEDITATION, you become like a mountain. You are surrounded by movement and changes, but you remain just as still and strong. Your thoughts would then be like clouds that float over you. They are there but you do not interact with them; they merely pass you by until they fade away into the distance.

MINDFULNESS MEDITATION in the formal sense can be practiced daily, but just like exercise and eating you need to set aside a specific time for it. However, unlike the first two, you do not have to change into a different set of clothes or prep some ingredients to practice. You can start anywhere and anytime.

. . .

How to Apply **the Right Meditation Posture**

It is important to make sure that you follow proper posture while being still for several minutes. Here are the steps on how to properly position yourself for meditation.

Sitting on a chair

Sitting still for an extended time requires good posture not only for health, but for comfort as well. Slouching, after all, is the surest way to cause long term damage on your spinal cord. Here are some tips on how to improve your sitting posture for meditation:

- Make sure to sit on a chair that will enable you to put your feet flat on the ground. If the chair is too low or high, you would be better off sitting on the floor.

- If you have a slouching problem, you can place wooden blocks or old magazines beneath the two back legs of your chair to allow it to tilt forward slightly. This slight tilt will compel you to maintain a straight back in order to keep balance.

- Visualize that you have a string pulling your stomach forward until your spine is naturally straight without any feeling of strain. Allow your head to lift naturally until all the discs in your spine are naturally aligned.

- You may place your hands on your knees. They can be facing downwards, upwards, or to the side. You can also place a cushion on your lap and place your hands on top if you feel tension on your shoulders.

SITTING **on the floor**

The more traditional and formal sitting practice for meditation is on a cushion on the floor. There are two basic postures for that: the kneeling posture and the Burmese posture. It is best to invest in a good quality meditation stool with a flat cushion (called a zafu) on top so that it can absorb the pressure of your weight instead of the back of your legs.

To properly do the kneeling posture, here are some tips:

- Always shake and stretch your legs as well as rotate your ankles before you go to the kneeling posture. This will minimize feelings of tension or strain.

- Prepare the kneeling stool and cushion on the floor, then carefully sit back down on it. Shift your weight until it is evenly distributed.

- Gently straighten your back and place your hands on your knees or lap.

TO DO THE BURMESE POSTURE, here are the steps:

- Do some stretching exercises for the legs to prepare them for the position.

- Lay out a mat or blanket on the floor. Over it, place a firm, flat cushion on which you will be sitting.

- Carefully lower yourself over the cushion into a sitting position. Try to let your knees to touch the floor; if they do not, you may need to add more cushions until they do.

- Let your left heel touch or be as close to your right inner thigh as possible. Let your right leg be in front of your left leg with its heel directed at the lower left leg. You do not have to position this perfectly, so adjust according to what is comfortable and stable for you.

- Gently allow your back to become straight, but with your shoulders relaxed. You may then place your hands on your knees or on a cushion on your lap.

ASIDE FROM FOLLOWING PROPER POSTURE, it is important to make sure to meditate during the times when you are not hungry or too full. Otherwise, you will be too distracted or sleepy.

THAT SAID, let us move on to one of the most fundamental mindfulness meditations, mindful breathing.

MINDFUL BREATHING MEDITATION

. . .

MINDFUL BREATHING MEDITATION is the core of all mindfulness meditation exercises. It is in fact the first thing you usually do to enter the state of mindfulness before you proceed with walking mindfulness, eating mindfulness, and other mindfulness exercises.

BEGINNERS ARE HIGHLY ENCOURAGED to practice this every day for at least two weeks so that they could get into the habit of meditation.

If you do not want to get lost in time or be worried about how long you are meditating, you can set a timer on your phone or alarm clock to signal you when to come out of the meditation. It is best to set a gentle tone on the alarm instead of a ringing one, as you would want the reminder to be gentle rather than a disturbance. You can start with 10 minutes, if you like.

Here are the steps to mindful breathing meditation:

STEP 1: Get yourself into a comfortable sitting posture, be it in a chair or on the floor. Give yourself time to become stable and comfortable.

STEP 2: When you are ready, announce to yourself and the universe that you are ready to focus on the present moment. You may start by saying out loud, "I am in the present moment. I am ready to meditate." Invite an attitude of kindness, curiosity, and acceptance.

STEP 3: Shift your focus towards your nostrils. Notice the feeling of your natural breath as you inhale through your nostrils. Then, trace the sensation of the breath as it flows down through your windpipe into your lungs, causing your belly to expand. Notice how it flows out of your belly, causing it to deflate, and then goes back up through your windpipe and nostrils. Continue to focus on this sensation for as long as you like.

BE careful not to change how you are breathing as your purpose here is not to judge how you are doing it. Rather, it is a mere observance of your natural breath, the core of your present moment.

STEP 4: As you continue to focus on your breath, you may soon notice your mind wandering off. This is completely normal and should not cause you to worry. All you need to do when you notice this happening is to draw your focus back towards your nostrils.

EACH TIME you start to entertain thoughts unrelated to the sensation of breath, call to mind the word "thinking..." You can also make it more specific, such as "worrying..." or "planning..." or "ruminating..." After the thought floats away, ground yourself back towards your breath.

ONCE YOU HEAR the timer go off, you can either gently come out of the meditation but bring the state of mindfulness with you throughout the rest of your day. Some like to shift their focus from their breath towards their surroundings after mindful breathing meditation. They focus on the colors, textures, and shapes, the sounds they hear, and so on. This enables them to become more in tune with the present moment than ever.

GUIDED meditation

. . .

THE MINDFULNESS MEDITATION practices may be difficult at first. It is recommended to try one of the apps or programs listed in the resources section to introduce you to meditation and help you with your posture, breathing and techniques. This will allow you to build a meditation habit with less than 10 minutes a day.

TRY PRACTICING mindful breathing meditation right now. If you don't have much time or can't sit down, just pause and take a few breaths in and out focus on your breath.

AFTER YOU ARE FINISHED, you might like to turn to the next chapter to learn another type of mindfulness meditation called Walking Mindfulness.

Mindfulness Exercise

Mindful Breathing

YOU CAN TRY short meditation and mindful breathing anywhere, you don't have to be sitting down to try it.

TO START FOCUS on breathing in through your nose and focus on the air going in at your nostrils, just focus on this point. Then breath out through your mouth, focus on the air just as it leaves your lips.

COUNT 1 when you breathe in and 2 when you breathe out, keep counting until 10.

.   .   .

YOU CAN ALSO TRY the full mantra from the smiling meditation mentioned earlier in the book or just the first 2 lines as you breathe in and out:

AS I BREATHE IN, my mind becomes calm.
	As I breathe out, my mind becomes clear.

LET GO OF THOUGHTS, worries and things you need to do and just focus on your breathing. You don't have to do this for very long but if you found it helpful, you can try for longer or do it a few times during the day as you feel you need to calm your mind a bit.

13

WALKING MINDFULNESS

"*Today, you can decide to walk in freedom. You can choose to walk differently.*
You can walk as a free person, enjoying every step."
Thich Nhat Hanh

HAVE you ever gone on a long walk to de-stress? If you have, then surely you know how therapeutic it is. Walking mindfulness is exactly that. It is an active form of meditation that also serves as a simple way to refresh and calm the mind.

THE BIGGEST DIFFERENCE between walking mindfulness and just plain walking, however, is that you allow your mind to focus on the present moment instead of your own thoughts and ideas while you are in the process of walking. Your purpose throughout the meditation is to enjoy the path itself rather than to merely use the path to solve a problem or let go of worries.

.   .   .

THE PROCESS of Walking Mindfulness

IT IS important to set aside at least 10 minutes for walking mindfulness as well as to choose where you will practice it. It can be as simple as an early morning walk around a peaceful neighborhood or a late afternoon walk at the park.

ONCE YOU HAVE DECIDED on that, here are the steps to follow:

Step 1: Stand upright at the starting point of the location that you have chosen for your walking mindfulness meditation. Aim for a posture that combines balance and confidence. Release any tension from your shoulders and arms, allowing the arms to hang to the sides in a natural way.

STEP 2: Begin by focusing on your nostrils and the breath that flows into them. Continue to focus on your breath for a few minutes.

STEP 3: When you are ready, lift your left foot and then notice the shift in your weight. Focus on the movement of your left foot as it steps forward, taking in any change of sensations to your whole body. Then, move your weight to take another step forward with your right foot. Keep in mind the sensations felt with each step.

STEP 4: Keep your focus on your body just for a few steps, ensuring that you are doing it in a place where there are no potential threats. Once you have assumed your natural way of walking, you can shift your focus towards your surroundings.

. . .

STEP 5: Allow your senses to take in all the stimuli around you. Notice the details – what you see, hear, smell, and touch – in a curious and open way. When thoughts unrelated to this present moment enter your mind, stop walking in a safe spot and then allow these thoughts to run their course without engaging in them.

ONCE THESE THOUGHTS start to fade away, draw your focus back towards your walk and then move forward and shift your focus towards your surroundings. Keep walking and savoring the journey in and of itself until you have reached your intended destination.

IT'S important not to listen to an audiobook, or music when practicing walking mindfulness but to take in all the sounds and be fully focused on your environment.

WALKING mindfulness allows you to appreciate not just your ability to walk, but also the surroundings in which you are walking. It is a great meditation to do when you are travelling in another place or simply expressing gratitude towards where you are. The next time you decide to enjoy going out on a stroll or sightseeing in another city, practice walking mindfulness and you are certain to make it a nourishing experience to the mind, body, and spirit.

Mindfulness exercise

Take a mindful walk in nature

THE PROCESS and steps for walking mindfulness are outlined in this chapter. We've also covered the benefits of being in nature.

.   .   .

THE EXERCISE for this chapter is to follow the steps outlined for walking mindfulness, remembering to take in all the details and not distract yourself with music, audiobooks, thoughts or worries.

IT DEPENDS on the season and where you live but as an added benefit try to take this mindful walk amongst nature - this could be a park or anywhere where you can be surrounded by nature.

14

MINDFUL EATING AND DRINKING

"Drink your tea slowly and reverently, as if it is the axis on which the world earth revolves - slowly, evenly, without rushing toward the future." - Thich Nhat Hanh

WE CANNOT HELP but eat and drink each day to stay alive. Sadly, though, many people pay little attention to the quality of their meals and beverages. They also tend to preoccupy themselves with other things, such as a television show, during their meals. This causes many to take their food, drink, and body for granted. In fact, eating mindlessly causes one to overeat and, when done repeatedly over the years, that person would then become obese and unhealthy.

THE GOOD NEWS is that you can end the habit of mindless eating by practicing its direct opposite – mindful eating. It is a kind of meditation, so to speak, since you would be focusing on one thing alone, and it is your meal. In other words, you will engage your senses, thoughts, and emotions towards the meal served in front of you.

. . .

MINDFUL EATING MAKES you become more appreciative of your food and it also makes you more conscious of the quality of the food served in front of you. Multiple studies, such as those published in the 2011 issue of *Eating Disorders* and the 2009 issue of *Appetite,* reveal that mindful eating can reduce overeating (thus leading to weight loss) and help those with eating disorders overcome their condition.

THE STEPS to Mindful Eating and Drinking

STARTING TODAY, you can build the habit of mindful eating and drinking. The secret to doing it successfully is by planning ahead of time. By preparing what you need before you start to crave for food or drink, you are a lot less likely to eat unhealthy food mindlessly.

TO HELP YOU BEGIN, here are the steps you should follow to practice mindful eating and drinking:

STEP 1: Create a fixed schedule for your meals as well as the places where you would be eating your meals.

It is always best to eat your meals at the table because it compels you to focus on your food. Eating at a desk or in front of the television will certainly keep you from being mindful of your meals.

STEP 2: Carefully select the foods you want to eat.

A variety of fresh, unprocessed, natural food such as meats, vegetables, fruits, nuts are the key to ensure that your body will be well nourished and fully satisfied after each meal. Be as careful of the serving portions as the quality of the food itself.

· · ·

STEP 3: Come up with a mindful eating ritual.

Human beings thrive on rituals. These patterns in our mind make us feel secure in what we are doing, and when we have a ritual to invite the attitude of mindful eating and drinking, we will become more inclined towards enjoying and paying full attention to the meal itself.

FOR INSTANCE, you could start by laying down all the items you need on the table: fork, spoon, knife, plate, glass, and so on. After you have laid them out, you can then add the food on the plate. Next, you sit down and express a prayer of gratitude for the meal. Finally, you spread your napkin on your lap and begin eating mindfully.

STEP 4: Engage the five senses as you eat and/or drink.

Before you take your first bite or sip, take a good look at the food or drink in front of you first. Notice the shape, size, color, and smell of it. Then, as you take it into your mouth, notice the flavor, texture, and the sound of it as it engages with your tongue and teeth. Slowly chew the food or swish the drink inside your mouth and savor the explosion of stimuli from it.

STEP 5: Take your time in eating mindfully and enjoy the entire process.

Spend at least twenty minutes with your meal, savoring each morsel and sip for as long as you like. Never rush through the dining experience because delicious and healthy food and thirst-quenching drinks should always be enjoyed.

TRY to practice mindful eating and drinking at every meal, even when you are just eating a small snack or drinking a glass of water to quench your thirst. By becoming conscious of what we put inside our bodies, we also become more inspired to take better care of it.

THINK OF IT THIS WAY: your mind serves as the gatekeeper to your digestive system, which serves as the gateway into your body. Make sure that your gatekeeper stays focused so that your body will be nourished with the right food and drink.

MINDFUL EATING INVOLVES BEING aware of the food you are putting in your body and focusing on the food as you are eating it. Focus on the smell of the food and its appearance. Eat slowly, observe the taste and the texture while chewing slowly and being present, without distractions from television or computers or anything else.

AN EXPERIENCE IN MINDFUL EATING:

If you live in a big city it's likely there is a restaurant experience where you can eat food in the dark. Being in darkness when eating your food, you remove distractions and concentrate more on the taste and texture of the food with heightened senses of smell and taste so you are much more mindful when eating.

YOU DON'T HAVE to have a restaurant to do this, you can do this just by closing your eyes when eating so you focus more on the taste and texture of the food.

MINDFUL EATING and mindfulness in relationships

. . .

IF YOU ARE in a relationship it's also a romantic idea for a mindful date to prepare a meal for another person that you both eat blindfolded or with your eyes closed and discuss the taste and sensations.

THIS IS ESPECIALLY interesting if the other person doesn't see the food and must guess the food as often our other senses cloud our judgement and they may have a completely different idea of what the food tastes like compared to you.

THIS EXPERIENCE in mindful eating in relationships generates conversation, distraction free eating and mindful time together as a couple while eating mindfully as well.

Mindfulness exercise

Mindful Eating

MINDFUL EATING HAS a lot of benefits as demonstrated in the steps outlined for mindful eating in this chapter.

FOR THIS EXERCISE just try mindful eating for one meal. Be mindful of the meal you chose and why you select it. Turn off phones and don't sit in front of TV or a computer while eating.

FIRST, focus on the smell of the food and its appearance. Then eat slowly, observing the taste and the texture while chewing slowly. Close your eyes while chewing to focus on the sense of taste. Take the time to enjoy the meal and the experience of eating.

15

MINDFULNESS QUOTES

Words have a profound impact on the mind and spirit and that is why this chapter shares with you some powerful and inspirational quotes on mindfulness. As you read each one of these quotes, it helps to pause and reflect on the words shared by its author.

YOU CAN CHOOSE your favorite quote to be reminded of each day and write down the words on a piece of paper and then place it somewhere that is visible to you each day, such as your bathroom mirror or on your bedside table. Perhaps you can also read one quote per day and then spend some time absorbing the meaning and how it relates to your life in the present moment.

HERE ARE some quotes on mindfulness:

Do not dwell in the past, do not dream of the future, concentrate the mind on the present moment.

(Buddha)

*Mindfulness is simply being aware of what is happening right now
without wishing it were different;
enjoying the present without holding on when it changes
(which it will);
being with the unpleasant without fearing it will always be this way
(which it won't).*
(James Baraz)

*Respond; don't react.
Listen; don't talk.
Think; don't assume.*
(Raji Lukkoor)

If you miss the present moment, you miss your appointment with life.
(Thich Nhat Hanh)

*The only thing that is ultimately real about your journey is the step that
you are taking at this moment. That's all there ever is.*
(Eckhart Tolle)

*With mindfulness, you can establish yourself in the present in order to
touch the wonders of life that are available in that moment.*
(Thich Nhat Hanh)

Surrender to what is. Let go of what was.
Have faith in what will be.
(Sonia Ricotti)

You cannot control the results, only your actions.
(Allan Lokos)

Stop, breathe, look around
and embrace the miracle of each day,
the miracle of life.
(Jeffrey A. White)

Stay present for the "now" of your life. It's your "point of power."
(Doug Dillon)

Paradise is not a place; it's a state of consciousness
(Sri Chinmoy)

Life is not lost by dying; life is lost minute by minute, day by
dragging day, in all the small uncaring ways.
(Stephen Vincent Benet)

If you aren't in the moment, you are either looking forward to
uncertainty, or back to pain and regret.
(Jim Carrey)

Begin at once to live, and count each separate day as a separate life.
(Seneca)

Sometimes you need to sit lonely on the floor in a quiet room in order to
hear your own voice and not let it drown in the noise of others.
(Charlotte Eriksson)

The real meditation is how you live your life.
(Jon Kabat-Zinn)

Mindfulness has helped me succeed in almost every dimension of my life.
By stopping regularly to look inward and become aware of my mental state,
I stay connected to the source of my actions and thoughts and can guide
them with considerably more intention.
(Dustin Moskovitz)

Most of us take for granted that time flies, meaning that it passes too
quickly. But in the mindful state, time doesn't really pass at all. There is
only a single instant of time that keeps renewing itself over and over with
infinite variety.
(Deepak Chopra)

Mindfulness isn't difficult. We just need to remember to do it.
(Sharon Salzberg)

In the end, just three things matter:
How well we have lived
How well we have loved
How well we have learned to let go
(Jack Kornfield)

In this moment, there is plenty of time. In this moment, you are precisely as
you should be. In this moment, there is infinite possibility.
(Victoria Moran)

Mindfulness is about love and loving life. When you cultivate this love, it
gives you clarity and compassion for life, and your actions happen in
accordance with that.
(Jon Kabat-Zinn)

Mindfulness Exercise

Pick a quote that resonates with you

THERE ARE a lot of quotes about mindfulness there, so pick one that
you feel applies to you and will benefit you in your day to day life.

· · ·

THINK about this quote and where it could help you be more mindful. What times during the day or your life could it be helpful for you to be reminded of this?

WRITE down the quote and put it somewhere that will help you be reminded of it when it will be helpful to you.

16

MINDFULNESS APPS AND RESOURCES

Mindfulness gives you time.
Time gives you choices.
Choices, skilfully made, lead to freedom.
You don't have to be swept away by your feeling.
You can respond with wisdom and kindness rather than habit and
reactivity.
(Henepola Gunaratana)

I n this chapter, you will be introduced to a variety of mindfulness apps and online resources that can help you build the habit of being mindful.

MANY OF THE mindfulness apps have similar features, however some are designed more for meditation, or for reducing anxiety and stress so it's worth considering what you are looking for when trying to introduce mindfulness into your day.

. . .

IF YOU CONSTANTLY FEEL OVERWHELMED and stressed and feel too busy to meditate then an app that sends a message during the day to remind you to breathe and be calm might be a good start.

IF YOU DON'T FEEL overwhelmed constantly but you may occasionally find your mind racing or have trouble focusing on your work or study then a meditation app might be more useful. This may help you plan your day and gain clarity, start building focus to reduce distractions, be more mindful of the task you are working on and concentrate on the tasks you are doing.

Mindfulness Apps

STOP BREATHE THINK

Stop Breathe Think is a mindfulness and meditation app run by a non-profit organization. The aim of the app is to inspire all people to develop kindness and compassion and live happier, less stressed lives.

THE WEBSITE and app are both very well presented and very easy to use. You can track your mood and meditation progress, along with rewards and encouragement as you move towards more a more mindful life.

STOP BREATHE THINK HELPS you take a few minutes each day to experience calm in your life. It has recommendations on sessions based on your mood. If you are feeling anxious or stressed, the app will recommend a different session than if you are unable to sleep.

SMILING Mind

Smiling Mind is a free app also run by a non-profit organization.

The app has a range of lessons to help build more mindfulness into your day.

SMILING Mind has a mission to provide accessible tools for mindfulness and meditation to reduce stress and the challenges of everyday life.

THEIR MINDFULNESS PROGRAMS have been co-developed with health, brain and psychology experts. The app is free and is available to anyone around the world making it accessible to develop mindfulness into your everyday life.

SMILING Mind also offers meditation lessons for children and teenagers as well as adults. The lessons on mindfulness are tailored for specific ages groups.

SMILING Mind is narrated with an Australian accent, so when selecting guided mindfulness or meditation programs it's important to select an accent and voice that you find calming and easy to understand.

SMILING Mind is free and is an excellent app and resource for learning to be more mindful every day.

THE MINDFULNESS APP

The Mindfulness app is another popular app to develop mindfulness and meditation habits.

.   .   .

You can choose from guided meditation or meditation in silence and set the duration of the meditation session. There is also an option to select the ringing of a bell at different intervals during the meditation.

There is the option to set reminders during the day to check whether you are being mindful and remind you to be present and focus on the moment.

There is also the option for daily reminders to meditate at certain times of the day, which can be helpful in building a meditation habit. This app also has a statistics section, keeping track of your progress over time.

Buddhify

Buddhify is a great app for starting to introduce mindfulness into your life. It has short guided mindfulness sessions that are specifically targeted towards activities such as household chores or feelings such as being stressed, having trouble sleeping or traveling etc.

Many of the guided tapes are a few minutes long so they are quick and easy to use at any time during the day to bring mindfulness into your life.

Buddhify is a one-off purchase, there are no ongoing monthly subscription fees and it is highly recommended.

Headspace

Headspace is a full training and education program to bring 10 minutes of guided meditation and calm into each day.

IT IS subscription based but there are 10 free lessons with videos explaining meditation and mindfulness.

IT ALLOWS you to connect with your friends and it has challenges to encourage each other to meditate daily.

WHILE IT IS A PAID monthly subscription it does contain a lot of value and content. It is based around building a meditation habit which is related to mindfulness but if you are interested in bringing mindfulness to your day without building a meditation habit then some of the other recommended apps may be more relevant especially at the start.

CALM

Calm is like headspace in that it has daily 10-minute meditation sessions; however, there are a number of differences that might make Calm a preferred choice for mindfulness compared to Headspace which is very meditation focused.

CALM OFFERS both guided and unguided meditation, it also has sounds from nature that you can listen to while meditating. Calm offers specific sessions like Buddify, such as walking mindfulness and sessions focused around feelings and emotions along with brain training for focus and concentration.

. . .

YOU CAN ADJUST the length of time you want to meditate or practice mindfulness. They even have sessions as short as 2 minutes to calm your mind and relax that you can start at any time of the day. This is a great way to introduce mindfulness into your day at any time.

ZENIFY

Zenify is very focused on incorporating mindfulness into each day. They state their mission is *"We believe that every person on this planet deserves to be happy. That's exactly why Zenify meditation and mindfulness app was created."*

THE APP PROVIDED simple reminders and suggestions on how to bring mindfulness into your life throughout the day. For example, you might get a reminder suggesting that you do whatever you are doing with your full attention and concentration which helps bring you back to focus on the task you are doing without distraction. Other reminders might be around awareness of the present moment and your emotions at the time.

THESE SUGGESTIONS and reminders cover different areas of life such as thoughts, emotions, friends, family, relationships and more. The app is free to try with a small one off cost to buy all the reminders and suggestions in the different areas of life.

THIS APP IS MUCH MORE mindfulness focused than meditation and is a good way to start introducing small amounts of mindfulness into your day.

CENTERED (CURRENTLY available in U.S.A only)

The centered app encourages you to incorporate mindfulness

into your day and allows you to track your activity and sessions. You can track how you are progressing to being more 'centered' and towards meeting your goals.

It also considers steps during the day, meditation sessions and syncs with Apple watch and the Apple health app to see how exercise and other factors contribute to your mood.

This allows you to live a more balanced 'centered' life mentally and physically, adding activities that contribute to a more positive mood and removing negative factors.

The app has specific mindfulness and meditation sessions for walking, compassion, exercise, and awareness. You can set daily steps and mindfulness/meditation goals and schedule these into your calendar and sync results with Apple health.

There is a lot of scientific research that has gone into the app in collaboration with hospitals, universities and psychology experts. If it is available in your local app store then it is worth considering as a mindfulness and health focused app.

NOTE: At the time of writing, the Centered app is currently only available in the U.S.A and may not be available in other countries yet.

Mindfulness daily

Mindfulness daily is another app with reminders and prompts to increase mindfulness in your daily life. It's often difficult to find time in the day to meditate or practice mindfulness, especially when stressed.

THIS APP PROVIDES quick guided mindfulness practices to reduce stress/anxiety, calm your mind and help improve your sleep. It has a pause button which you can press if you feel you are being overwhelmed by the day and pause for a short time and engage in some breathing exercises.

THE REMINDERS CAN BE SET at different times during the day to remind you to take some deep breaths and help you relax. The app is focused on being calm and reducing stress and anxiety. If you often feel overwhelmed and anxious then this app might be a good start before trying meditation and other apps to help first reduce anxiety and stress.

7 SECOND MEDITATION

This app is simple but effective if you are starting to introduce mindfulness into your day and feel you are too busy for meditation or other practices. The idea is that everyone has at least 7 seconds to a read a message during the day.

OFTEN, we receive messages and they cause us to be stressed and to be anxious so this app sends different messages during the day reminding us to pause for a moment, calm our thoughts, be present in the moment and experience how beautiful life is.

THE APP IS like getting a message from a friend that only takes a few seconds to read but the message makes you smile and puts you in a positive calm mood.

. . .

3 MINUTE mindfulness

The 3 Minute Mindfulness app aims to make mindfulness simple and easy to apply during your day with minimal time commitment.

THE APP IS DESCRIBED as "Mindfulness without the fluff" as it attempts to simplify mindfulness so it is understandable to everyone of all age ranges with no previous experience with meditation or mindfulness.

THE EXERCISES ARE ONLY three minutes, as the app name suggests, so it's easy to do these exercises regardless of how busy your day is.

THE APP HAS mindfulness reminders that prompt you throughout the day to be more mindful, along with a range of short 3-minute meditation and mindfulness exercises that you can practice whenever you get these reminders or you find your day becoming too stressful or your mind racing with thoughts. It also connects to the iPhone health app to record the time you spent practicing mindfulness each day.

MINDFULNESS WEBSITES

Many of the apps mentioned above also have websites where you can use their programs through any computer if you don't have a smartphone or prefer to use the website.

THE WEBSITES for the apps mentioned above that also have web based apps are:

. . .

HEADSPACE:
   www.headspace.com

CALM:
   www.calm.com

STOP BREATH THINK:
   www.stopbreathethink.org

SMILING MIND:
   www.smilingmind.com.au

THERE ARE ALSO a range of other website and resources about mindfulness that are worth considering for learning more about mindfulness:

MINDFUL (MINDFUL.ORG)
   This quintessential mindfulness website provides you with a variety of self-help posts on how to practice being mindful at work as well as in your personal life.

THE AMERICAN MINDFULNESS **Research Association (goamra.org)**
   Those who wish to learn more about the scientific aspect of mindfulness can visit this site to gain access to plenty of studies regarding the subject.

ZEN HABITS (ZENHABITS.COM)

This minimalist mindfulness blog provides you with practical tips and inspiring posts on how to live a happy, mindful, and simple life.

Tiny Buddha (tinybuddha.com)

This website provides you not only with blog posts about mindfulness, health, and inspiration from Buddhism, but also gives you access to forums to communicate with those who wish to practice living in the present moment as well.

THE MINDFULNESS PROJECT (londonmindful.com)

This blog serves as a platform for sharing practical techniques and insights into mindfulness, and it includes expert advice from a team of mindfulness gurus based in Central London.

THERE ARE plenty of other wonderful apps and online resources aside from these suggestions that you can try at home. Don't try them all at once, but read about what might be suitable, find the ones that work best for your needs and use them to help you establish the habit of being mindful each day.

Mindfulness Exercise

Practice a guided mediation session

FROM THE LIST of meditation and mindfulness apps, pick one and sign up to it.

SCHEDULE SOME TIME into your day, even if it's only 10 minutes, and practice one of the guided meditation sessions from the app.

. . .

IF YOU HAVE SELECTED a mindfulness app or website, try one of the mindfulness exercises during that time.

SCHEDULE THE TIME in your day to be a regular time of peace and calm where you will practice meditation and mindfulness.

START with one session for around 10 minutes and see if you can build it into a daily habit.

AFTERWORD

"Now is the future that you promised yourself last year, last month, last week.

Now is the only moment you'll ever really have.

Mindfulness is about waking up to this."

- Mark Williams

Now that you have reached the end of this book, the last step to take is to apply mindfulness in your life each day. You do not have to apply all the lessons that you have learned from this book right away. Rather, it is best to introduce one small habit at a time.

It's also crucial to understand where you are on your journey to mindfulness, if you are currently experiencing depression, stress, anxiety or panic attacks then it's important to seek professional guidance first before trying mindfulness techniques. Mindfulness and meditation are best as a management strategy, not as a stand-alone initial treatment strategy.

Starting small on the areas of your life where you need to introduce more mindfulness is a great way to start. Mindfulness is a keystone habit, once you start to introduce mindfulness in one area of your life it will have effects that flow into other areas of your life.

If you are in a relationship and feel in a rut or that you aren't communicating or spending much time together, then you can start by using some of the mindfulness techniques in the chapter about mindfulness in relationships.

If work is causing you a lot of stress and you feel you are constantly busy and not getting anything done, then introducing techniques in the chapter on mindfulness at work can help you in this area.

Pick a small technique to start, this could be just taking a deep breath and pausing for a few seconds during the day.

You can then build on that initial habit by going for a walk and incorporating mindfulness into it or applying mindful eating and drinking at least during dinnertime, if not in each meal.

How you start to establish your own mindfulness routine is entirely up to you. Small changes will ultimately lead to a significant difference and improvement in your life.

Keep practicing and, eventually, you will come to realize that you are a lot more in tune with yourself, with others, and with your surroundings because of it. Each tiny step towards becoming more mindful will build upon each other until it is easy to find calm and mindfulness in each day.

PLEASE LEAVE A REVIEW

If you enjoyed this book, found issues or wanted to get in contact:

If you appreciated the information provided in this book, please take a few moments to share your opinions and post a review on Amazon and view other books at the link here:

https://www.amazon.com/author/mindfulnessmeditation

I would be very grateful for you in your support if you found this book useful.

If you have any feedback, found any errors in the book or just wanted to get in contact to say hi, please feel free to email me at: gshaw-books@gmail.com

Thank you for reading this book, I hope you have found the information useful and it helps introduce mindfulness into your life bringing you more calm and happiness every day.

"The present moment is filled with joy and happiness. If you are attentive, you will see it."

Thich Nhat Hanh

ABOUT THE AUTHOR

Gabriel Shaw has lived in Asia for over 5 years, studying meditation, mindfulness and Buddhist teachings.

He was working in an office job and found himself stressed, over-worked and unhappy. His health deteriorated and he sustained a back injury that left him in bed for weeks, with pain shooting through his body if he moved.

He was forced to leave his job and spent months recovering, it was during this time he discovered yoga, Pilates, meditation and mind-fulness.

These practices made a huge impact in his recovery when almost everything else he tried failed. He continued these methods and found significant improvements in his health, mind and life.

He then moved to Asia to study these practices in great depth and immerse himself in understanding these teaching and philosophies.

He has studied under Buddhist monks in temples throughout South East Asia and brings those experiences and lessons to his teachings.

Currently he lives in Thailand and practices daily meditation and mindfulness.

He hopes to pass on this knowledge of mindfulness, meditation and other practical skills in an easy to understand and practical manner that you can apply in your everyday life.

"Be kind whenever possible.
Remember, it is always possible."
- Dalai Lama

ALSO BY GABRIEL SHAW

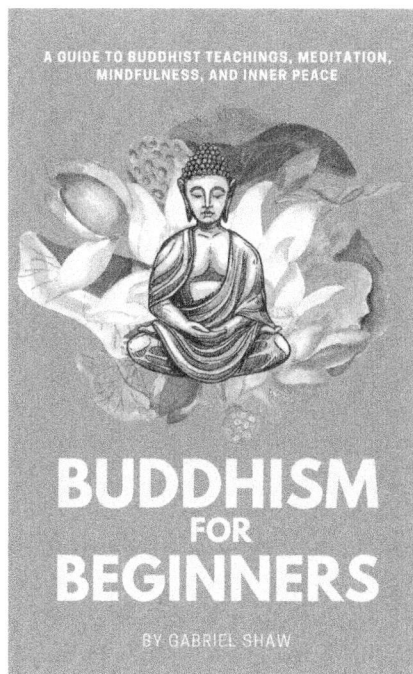

Buddhism for Beginners - Buy on Amazon

365 Buddhist Quotes - Buy on Amazon

Printed in Great Britain
by Amazon